Praise for

The Most Overlooked Women of the Bible

"Mary so beautifully intertwines storytelling and Biblical narrative to show God's kindness and faithfulness to fifteen extraordinary women. For these women knew the pain of being overlooked, yet God was present with and merciful to each of them. I found Mary's writing a great, tender gift—one that encouraged and ministered to me."

—**Laura Barringer**, co-author of *A Church Called Tov* and *Pivot: The Priorities, Practices, and Powers That Can Transform Your Church into a Tov Culture*

"In *The Most Overlooked Women of the Bible*, Mary DeMuth has beautifully rendered all-too-often forgotten women, unpacking their stories with wisdom, insight, and grace. Through her biblical accounts, we are reminded that we are not forgotten, trapped, or unseen in the presence of a good God who always remembers, frees, and sees us. This is the book I wish I'd had growing up in the church. It's one I'm grateful my daughter and congregation will!"

—**Rev. Courtney Ellis**, author of *Looking Up: A Birder's Guide to Hope Through Grief* and pastor at Presbyterian Church of the Master

"I love Mary's writing! *The Most Overlooked Women of the Bible* is a beautifully crafted exploration of the stories we often miss. Mary's retelling of these accounts reads like a novel, and then she adds in wonderful biblical insight and practical ways to apply these stories to our modern-day lives. This is a must-read for anyone looking to deepen their understanding of Scripture and draw wisdom from the unsung heroines of the Bible."

—**Rob Teigen**, Best-selling author, podcaster, and Co-Founder of Growing Home Together

"Prepare to be seen and heard! Open DeMuth's new book and you'll enter compelling portraits of Biblical women who overcame injustices, hurt and misogyny with stunning faith. You'll come away with a deepened sense of God's abiding presence and covenantal love, no matter your own circumstances. But more than this, she presents practical sage paths forward out of pain into healing and strength. DeMuth's prose, as always, is brilliant; the biblical wisdom she presents is timely and invaluable."

—**Leslie Leyland Fields**, author of *Nearing a Far God: Praying the Psalms with Our Whole Selves*

"Mary DeMuth brings the often-overlooked women of the Bible to life, offering a fresh, theologically rich perspective that invites both men and women to find healing, hope, and encouragement. Blending historical fiction with deep biblical insight, this book will inspire readers to engage with Scripture in a new and truly transformative way."

—**Daniel Gilman**, PhD Candidate, Faculty of History, University of Cambridge, Director of the Centre for Public Speaking, Legislative Advisor for the Interparliamentary Taskforce on Human Trafficking

"Radiant brilliance bringing the wisdom, hope, and comfort of Jesus, who sees, loves, and validates those who feel unseen by the world. Mary DeMuth will pastor you with challenge and tenderness in these pages. This is wonderfully worth your time, as we embrace the sufficiency of quiet, distinct, faithfulness."

—Rev. Dr. Johnny Douglas

"Hope shines brightly in Mary DeMuth's newest survey of women in the Bible. In the stories of women you likely skip over as you read, DeMuth offers us hope, purpose, and a vision for serving God. When the world doesn't notice us, we can be confident that God does, and that we have a place in his plan."

—Kelley Mathews, ThM

"Princess. Apostle. Grandmother. Prophet. Mother. Slave. Women in Scripture bearing these titles and more have one thing in common: they all loved God and are counted among *The Most Overlooked Women in the Bible*. Through a fictionalized retelling of these women's stories followed by reflections on the biblical text, Mary DeMuth beautifully explores what it means to live in seeming obscurity as a joyful servant of The God Who Sees."

—Dr. Sandra Glahn, seminary professor; general editor of *Vindicating the Vixens: Revisiting Sexualized, Vilified, and Marginalized Women of the Bible*; co-founder of the Visual Museum of Women in Christianity

The Most Overlooked WOMEN of the Bible

The MOST OVERLOOKED WOMEN *of the* BIBLE

What Their Stories Teach Us about Being Seen and Heard

MARY DEMUTH

REGNERY
FAITH

Author is represented by Joy Eggerichs Reed of Punchline Agency.

Regnery Faith™ is an imprint of Skyhorse Publishing, Inc.®, a Delaware corporation.

Visit our website at www.regnery.com.
Please follow our publisher Tony Lyons on Instagram
@tonylyonsisuncertain.

10 9 8 7 6 5 4 3 2 1

Library of Congress Cataloging-in-Publication Data is available on file.

Cover design by David Ter-Avanesyan
Cover photograph by Courtney Davis

Print ISBN: 978-1-5107-8225-9
eBook ISBN: 978-1-5107-8226-6

Printed in the United States of America

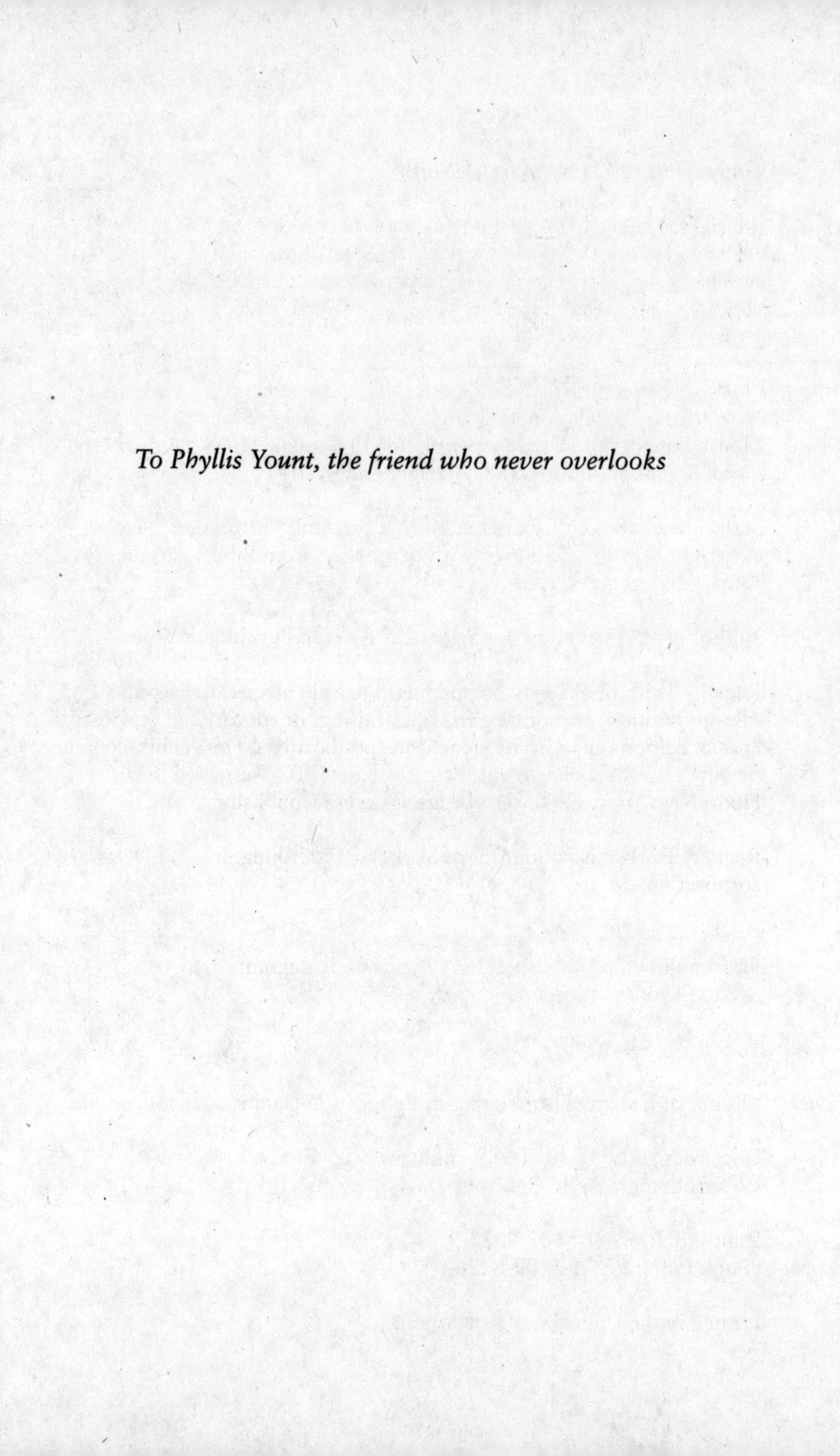

To Phyllis Yount, the friend who never overlooks

CONTENTS

Introduction

My life has been a series of lessons of trying to do "everything" right, yet not getting noticed for my efforts. I now know that I jumped through all those societal hoops precisely because I had a hole the size of Texas in my heart, shaped like the family that never could or would fulfill me. I wanted a mom and dad to love me, and since I was an only child (until my half-sister came along, though we never lived together), I looked for male and female connections in the landscape of schoolyard friendships. And yet, all that emptiness created a desperation for approval that never quite got satiated.

Can you relate?

As a rail-thin girl with zero athletic prowess, I grew accustomed to being picked last for kickball or any other sort of sport. In junior high, I hugged the wall at dances, watching all the popular girls slow dance with the boys who chose them. At my first and only (quite embarrassing) pageant, I watched as girls with lower grade-point averages got academic awards simply because they had "the look" and I did not. In high school, I envied any girl who had a boyfriend and wondered why God didn't love me enough to allow one. (Now I am grateful for that absence, but at the time I simply felt unnoticed and unworthy of attention.) In college, I tried on different identities, hoping one would garner the attention I desperately needed.

When I married and started having children, I expected this need for external approval inside me to subside. After all, I had what I had longed for all my life—a family, finally. But that insatiable desire to be seen remained, though it stagnated a bit amid diapers and young family life.

Pursuing publication didn't help matters any. In that world, you must don a thick hide to weather the barrage of rejections, further cementing that achy inner place that longs for acknowledgment. It's a treadmill going nowhere, a constant horizon that you never reach. I remember one interaction with a publisher early in my career. He shook my hand at an industry event. (He noticed me!) He released his grasp, looked me in the eyes, said, "We are so disappointed in your book sales," and then walked away. His sharp words and subsequent dismissal lingered in my heart for a long time. (Still does, if I'm honest.)

To be overlooked is to feel nullified, unseen, unheard. It creates an ache that's hard to overcome. And I believe it's knitted into the human condition. With so many of us jockeying for attention, it's no wonder there aren't many people left to give it. We're all so preoccupied with getting our own needs met that we fail to see that everyone else is hurting too.

We see this depicted in the New Testament in a powerful statement in Acts 6:1: "But as the believers rapidly multiplied, there were rumblings of discontent. The Greek-speaking believers complained about the Hebrew-speaking believers, saying that their widows were being *discriminated against* in the daily distribution of food" (emphasis mine). Those words, "discriminated against," are the Greek word *paratheoreo*—from *para*, which means "aside," and *theoreo*, which means "to contemplate or behold."

You can see where the word *theory* came from in the word's latter half. Have you ever had someone cling to an unfair theory about you? Then perhaps you've been *paratheoreo-d*! The Greek here means to "take a slight notice of."[1] There's an element of comparison in the phraseology—in other words, if you are comparing two people, one is overlooked because one doesn't measure up to the other. One is unserved, while the other "deserves" to be served.

But we don't need to have the precise word "overlooked" in the sacred text to realize there were many people throughout biblical history who felt the sting of comparison-found-wanting. Joseph comes to mind, as his own flesh and blood overlooked his humanity to sell him into slavery. David, the shepherd boy, was overlooked by his father when the prophet came to anoint one of his sons as the future king. Jeremiah, who wept his way through stern words for the nation of Israel, spent time in a cistern, unseen, as thanks for his unpopular prophecies. Jesus, coming from the no-name town of Nazareth, was underestimated, maligned, and dismissed by the very people he came to serve. The Apostle Paul wrote many letters defending his apostleship to those who seemed to relish dismissing him.

Of course, men aren't the only ones in the biblical narrative who were overlooked. Plenty of women were as well. How they navigated the dismissal they experienced and their feelings of being unnoticed are beautiful tutorials for us today. As I wrote in the first book of this series, *The Most Misunderstood Women of the Bible: What Their Stories Teach Us About Thriving*, we make the mistake of thinking the people in the Bible are characters, but not fully alive human beings with problems and angst just like us. They weren't superhuman; they were simply human. They weren't archetypes or stereotypes; they were plain types of folks. When we finally come to realize that the Bible is peopled with people just like us, it becomes both an encouragement and a cautionary tale of human behavior.

There is a plethora of overlooked women in the Bible, so writing this book became a challenge of selecting the right ones. I didn't want to reuse the same ten stories of women from my last book, though there is some overlap between being misunderstood and overlooked. I chose these women because, to me, their stories demonstrate being unseen or unheard, either by the people of their own time or by scholars who over the millennia have grossly underestimated them. I longed to give each of these women breath and life, to flesh them out so you feel like you know them. In the pages ahead, I'll do this through the power of story, relying heavily on the biblical text to frame each narrative as well as scholarship to help you understand their context and unique situations. Each chapter will start with a fictionalized historical account and end with the "so what" of their overlooked story: How does each story impact you as you're walking through your own overlooked journey? What can we all learn from these women's gritty responses to unfairness?

Together, we will learn about:

- Tamar of Judah, who desperately needed to extend her family line
- Miriam, who often faded into the background of Moses's grand story arc
- Zelophehad's daughters, who had to advocate for their very existence
- Deborah, who judged and guided an entire nation
- Abigail, whose marriage to Nabal certainly could've been her demise

- Jehosheba, who hid a king's heir and preserved the royal line of David
- Anna, the widowed prophetess who held baby Jesus
- Martha, the worried and bothered sister who busied herself with preparations for guests
- Grandma Lois and Mama Eunice, who loved and launched the Apostle Timothy
- Junia, the female apostle whose name was changed to Junias by early and late Bible scholars to pass her off as a male

I'm grateful to have this opportunity to walk alongside you. Picture me putting my arm around you (if you allow) and gently reminding you of the audacious way Jesus Christ truly saw and heard people. He demonstrated the heart of his Father to seek and save those who felt lost and isolated. He pursued the unpursued. He noticed the unnoticed. He heard the unheard. He saw the unseen. He dignified those society would deem undignified. He saw the mark of God's image in each person he encountered, and he continues to do that today. No matter how overlooked you may have felt in your childhood (or even last week), there is a Savior who absolutely sees you. Who delights in noticing you. Who will never, ever leave you or walk away.

Good stories have heroes. You'll encounter them throughout this book through the narratives of these plucky women. And you'll experience plenty of villains, too. But the greatest hero of the biblical story, by far, is Jesus of Nazareth, the one who understands being underestimated, unseen, and overlooked. He has deep empathy for you right now. And, according to Hebrews 7:25, "He lives forever to intercede with God on [your] behalf." He is *for* you, friend. He takes notice of your frailty, unspoken needs, and secret dreams for the future. He is good. And he wants a good life for you.

You are not the sum of the words spoken over you. Though you have walked through seasons of being overlooked, *paratheoreo* is not your reality. Even if all human beings picked you last for kickball, God chose you before the foundation of the world to bear fruit, live a life of abundance, and be filled by his ever-filling presence. I grieve with you for those eras of overlookedness. I acknowledge the sting and stink of that kind of treatment. I lament those seasons of feeling voiceless. They are real, as those experiences echo the realities of life in a very fallen world.

But they do not get to label you.

As I look back on those instances of living on the outside of polite (or not-so-polite) society, I can picture Jesus there, standing next to me, befriending me, even when I felt bereft of friendship or even the conviviality of a group of acquaintances. In my unaccepted state, he loved me. I may not have known it then, but I'm forever grateful that I'm grasping his acceptance and kindness toward me now.

Come adventure with me as we dive into the stories of women just like you who experienced the pain of being overlooked yet found a way to persevere. Who didn't allow the treatment of others to define who they were or how they lived. While others found them lacking by comparison to their peers, they clung to their Creator and took the next faithful step. That's my prayer for you—that you too will learn the value of walking alongside Jesus, who takes supreme notice of you, who died so you could experience relationship with him, and who understands the angst of being overlooked. "This High Priest of ours understands our weaknesses, for he faced all of the same testings we do, yet he did not sin" (Hebrews 4:15).

Jesus understands you. He understands your inner pain. He is here as you read this book.

CHAPTER ONE

Tamar, the Forgotten One

Her father-in-law seemed to live with a chip on his shoulder—being not the first, but the fourth child of an unloved woman. The firstborn meant more to their parents and to society, as did the children of the more beloved wife, as Tamar knew all too well. The pecking order of families with intricate liaisons and regulations meant she had little choice if she wanted to survive.

Survival. The word thrummed through her in the arid valley of waiting which seemed to stretch ahead of her like a pathway leading to a hidden cistern, open-mouthed and ready to devour her. She touched her wrist, the only part of her left untouched by the ravages of worry. It could not wrinkle the way her eyes did as she squinted in a search for elusive hope.

Tamar tasted wickedness during the first hiccups of her marriage to Judah's firstborn, Er. She began matrimony as most young girls did—with fear tinged with the kind of joy that comes when you realize your life is finally going to begin, no longer under the tutelage of parents, but as a woman carefully selected. But when she removed her wedding veil, and her eyes met Er's, her stomach turned. Er's eyes were cold and taunting as he spit her name. *Tamar*. As if her name never meant the sweetness of a date palm, as if he were uttering blasphemies and tasting bile.

She instinctively pulled away under their tent's canopy, the way one recoils from an asp. His cold shadow overcame her, and she shivered. She remembered the stories of old, of a wily serpent in the Garden bent on destroying everyone, and she feared she'd been married off to one of his wily servants. She soon became familiar with the sting of a slap across her face—and then it became normal. But worst? His words. Sentence upon sentence, he spat to demean her, she knew. His evildoing did not merely extend her way. His malevolent actions came from a bent heart that swindled even his relatives, all with a smile pasted on his black-bearded face.

The God of Covenant, she knew, heard the prayers of the desperate, and he became her only solace. Tamar's petitions became pleas without words, as if her heart prayed unintelligibly while her eyes leaked. The burden of being married to Er was far greater than the burden of life with her family of old. "Please," she prayed. "Please."

Tamar remembered the Hebrew stories of Hagar—the servant of Sarai who had been forsaken, bereft, and lost, yet God Almighty found her in the wilderness after she ran away. Like Hagar, Tamar bore the weight of being an outsider. While Hagar's was a wilderness of isolation, Tamar's desert was populated by an unpredictable jackal.

"Tamar!" came a roar from within their dwelling.

She knew that tone, felt it in her gut. She took in a long, heavy breath, steadying herself, then entered its dank belly.

What followed was the familiar tirade against her so-called barrenness, how weak-willed she was, how she was no better than a filthy, broken vessel.

"You are nothing!" Er roared. Though not much taller than she, the afternoon sun poured through the tent's mouth at such an angle that his shadow became a Nephilim, a menacing, angry giant. He drew near and spat in her face.

It was then that God saw fit to answer her pleas, her "please."

Er turned his taunts from Tamar to the Almighty himself, shaking his fist heavenward with vile, horrid words. Suddenly, Er's eyes widened as if he were seeing an apparition. With blasphemies still upon his sinister lips, he dropped to the ground, stone-cold dead, already stiffened.

When Judah saw his dead son, it seemed to come as no surprise. "He is Shua's son," he said to Tamar. "It's my wife's Canaanite blood coursing through his actions that's brought this about." He seemed resigned, as if he had always known this end would come, then took a deep breath. He motioned for Tamar to follow him into the light of day, away from death's stench.

She veiled herself, wondering why she felt nothing but relief at Er's demise.

"You know our Levirate Law, do you not?" Judah asked.

Tamar nodded.

"To carry on my line, I will give you to Onan. He will do his duty with you and provide the necessary offspring."

She shuddered. Er had been wicked, yes, but Onan was cut from the same familial fabric. Would her life be any different under his hand?

She retreated under a date palm, steadying her nerves, but she could still hear the conversation between Judah and Onan.

"No!" Onan spat. Though he said no more, Tamar knew his

meaning. He didn't want his brother's widow. She was not his preference.

"Go and marry Tamar," Judah said again, his voice firm but even, "as our law requires of the brother of a man who has died. You must produce an heir for your brother."

Onan spat upon the ground, stalking back and forth until he'd worn a pathway through the sand. But eventually, he obeyed.

No one wants to be the last choice, Tamar reasoned as she tried to empathize with Onan. In the marriage tent, she dared to hope that once her belly swelled, his disposition would change. But that chance never arrived; every time they had relations, he would withdraw, spilling their potential for children on the marriage bed.

Tamar's desperate pleas to the Almighty turned sour. What hope did she have in a world bent on depriving her of heirs? And how could she endure another man's wrath-filled eyes? Having once again satisfied himself without satiating her womb, Onan looked down upon her. "I despise you," he said.

Two days later, God spilled Onan's life. His death was not like Er's sudden one, but a rapid wasting away from vitality to grayed skin and sharply inhaled breaths that suddenly collapsed in a rattle.

When Judah laid eyes on his second dead son, he turned again to Tamar. Though he said nothing of the sort, she felt his judgment. The common thread between the two deceased brothers (Judah's best hope for lineage!) was her. He must've felt she was the curse that killed them.

She wanted to say something, anything, to turn his dark thoughts toward the light, but she said nothing.

Judah, once again, asked her to leave the tent.

She veiled herself and squinted against the hot, relentless sun. All she wanted was to lie on the earth in her dwelling and try to discern how to best move forward. After all, the third brother of Er and

Onan, Shelah—her rightful third husband under the Levirite Law—was but a boy. Perhaps Judah would shelter her until he was old enough to marry—but something told her this would not happen.

Judah cleared his throat, coughed. He wiped sweat from his brow, then grabbed his bearded chin. He turned away from her. "Go back to your parents' home," he said, "and remain a widow until my son Shelah is old enough to marry you."

"But—" Tamar wanted to say more, wanted to plead her case of needing to stay here to ensure she'd be married to Shelah, but she knew the futility of guarantees like that. She let her interjection hang in the afternoon air, unspoken.

Tamar gathered what little she had and, like Hagar, ventured into the wilderness toward what used to be her home. She spent the long journey with the words *barren* and *bereft* echoing through her mind. She would be a widow now. Spoiled for marriage. Destined to live out her years childless and unable to provide for herself or her parents.

When she arrived home, her head hung low, and she did not raise her eyes or even explain what had happened. She donned mourning clothes and said nothing.

Years passed. Tamar's mourning did not. She continued to wear the garments of a widow, and she would do so until God orchestrated a reversal.

Despite the kindness of her parents and siblings, it was painful to watch each sibling marry and produce heirs and, thus, security. Her only solace became her faith in a God who opened barren wombs and executed judgment on the wicked. Surely, he could see her plight. But even beyond her grief, a fierce fidelity arose in her.

Her people needed to continue, generation after generation. Hadn't God told Father Abraham that his descendants would become as numerous as specks of sand in the desert or the stars in the night sky? Judah should have been zealous to ensure that his firstborn's legacy would continue, to be a part of the sand-and-star promise. Yet since his son Shelah had finally reached marrying age and Tamar had not been summoned, she could only reason that Judah despised doing what was right—not only for him, but for all their people. Why wouldn't he do the right thing?

Rumor came that Judah, too, had become a widower.

And then? An opening. A small light.

One of Tamar's servants, Noa, entered her dwelling, opening the flap to let the sun's rays sweep through the tent. Dust particles danced in the descending light. "Look," Noa said. "Your father-in-law is going up to Timnah to shear his sheep."

"Please allow me some privacy," Tamar told her.

At once she removed her widow's garments and freshened her face. She donned brightly colored clothes she had not allowed herself to wear, then veiled her face. Unchaperoned, Tamar made her way to the village of Enaim, her heart thrumming with each step. Enaim was the gateway to Timnah, and Judah would have to pass through its center to get there. The closer she neared the town, the more resolve she felt rising in her soul. If Judah would not do the right thing of his own accord, she would compel him.

Weary from the journey, she sat beside the road to Enaim's entrance, still veiled. Many hours passed as she watched for her father-in-law's familiar gait. Squinting through her veil, she finally spied him, noticing the familiar stoop of his shoulder.

Judah, eyes hungry from the forced celibacy of widowerhood, looked at Tamar's bright clothes and her position at the side of the road—the place where prostitutes were known to gather.

Her heart quickened. What if he knew who she was? What would be her punishment for doing this? Would he whip off her veil, ruining her plan?

She said nothing, kept her eyes to the earth. Prayed. Reminded herself of Hagar, who was seen by God.

Judah stopped, his gaze fixed on her. He looked around and cleared his throat. "Let me have sex with you," he said plainly. His was not a voice of longing, but of demand and expectation.

Tamar swallowed. "How much will you pay to have sex with me?" she asked.

He paused, considering. "I'll send you a young goat from my flock," he said finally.

Typical. This is a man who does not keep his promises, she reasoned. *He says many things, but he does not follow through on his words.* Something rose up within her, steadying her voice. "But what will you give me to guarantee that you will send the goat?" she asked.

She could see the shadow of frustration cross his countenance. He rolled his eyes to the heavens. "What kind of guarantee do you want?"

A fly landed on her tunic. She flicked it away. It then landed on his sandal, but he did not shake it off.

"Leave me your identification seal and its cord and the walking stick you are carrying." Tamar felt her heartbeat in her fingertips as she congratulated herself for asking for so much. Women were given little in Israel, though the good Lord had commanded the people to have compassion on widows. Unfortunately, her status as a widow had not garnered tangible care from her community, just pity.

She wondered if Judah would comply, but she did not have to speculate long.

He handed the seal, its cord, and his walking stick to her, and then led her to a secluded area off the road.

He wasted no time with his desire. And then, unlike Onan who refused to consummate, Judah finished with a sigh, leaving her in haste.

As Tamar ventured home, she knew her womb had welcomed Judah's act. Her stomach roiled, even then, as if she were rocking on a boat being battered by waves. She removed her veil when she entered her tent, then donned the familiar widow's clothing. She buried the seal and its cord in the corner of her tent and propped the walking stick nearby.

And then she waited.

It was Noa who nonchalantly brought news three months later as Tamar's belly swelled, recounting Judah's story of asking Hirah the Adullamite to give a young goat to the prostitute he had encountered in Enaim so he could recover the things he'd given her. "Hirah could not find her," Noa said. "He kept asking for the shrine prostitute who sat beside the road at Enaim's entrance."

Noa looked knowingly in Tamar's direction. "They said they'd never had a shrine prostitute there. And Hirah told Judah he could not find the woman anywhere. Apparently, there's never been a shrine prostitute sitting at that particular place."

Noa paced to the tent's corner, then touched the walking stick. Tamar's rollicking stomach soured. *She knows*.

Of course, everyone in her small clan knew she was carrying a child, but no one (she thought) knew the how or the why of it because Tamar had kept deathly quiet. Even so, rumors had an insidious way of traveling through the clan.

"Judah said the prostitute could keep his things because he

didn't want to appear a fool to the townspeople," Noa said, continuing to caress the walking stick. "And just now Judah heard of your state. Someone said you'd acted like a prostitute and are carrying a child."

Tamar instinctively cradled her belly in her hands.

"He's demanded you be brought out publicly and burned to death. It's only a matter of time, as his men are now approaching our village."

As Noa finished speaking, several men entered Tamar's tent without invitation or permission. One grabbed her forearm and dragged her into the daylight of scrutiny. "You must come with us, harlot!"

Tamar tried to calm her panic, and then remembered what she had buried like treasure beneath her bed—and why she had asked for it in the first place.

"What is all this?" Tamar's father demanded of the mob.

"Your pregnant daughter has played the prostitute, and now, by decree of Judah, we must bring her to him to be burned!" they said.

Tamar's father, who already knew of her disgrace, turned redfaced but said nothing.

"Stop!" she cried. "Before you drag me to Judah, convey a message to him."

"What message is this?" the one who nearly tore her arm from her shoulder spat.

"If you let go of me, I'll show you."

The man released his grip, and she told them to wait. She grabbed the walking stick, then used it to unearth Judah's seal and cord from beneath her bed. She brought the items out to the group under the gaze of the relentless sun.

"What are these?" one of the men asked.

She presented all three items as if they were an offering. "The man who owns these things made me pregnant. Look closely."

The men drew near, and she told herself to steady the wild beat of her heart.

"Whose seal and cord and walking stick are these?" she demanded.

None of the men spoke.

The first man grabbed them in the same angry manner he had grabbed Tamar, said nothing, and left, with the rest of the group following in his wake.

A few days later, the men returned—not with violence this time, but an invitation. One told her, "Judah told us this when we returned his possessions to him: 'She is more righteous than I am, because I didn't arrange for her to marry my son Shelah.'" They motioned for her to go with them so she could live under the protection of Judah and his family.

Once again, Tamar left her home with hope, wondering if this time her tragedy would turn triumphant—or at least protected. As she trudged toward Judah's village, the baby within her quickened. She may have ventured to Judah's domain naïvely the first time considering the weight of the evil Er and Onan would commit against her, but now she bore the future of Israel's legacy within her.

When Tamar's belly ripened past due and the waters within her doused the earth, the midwife instructed her to breathe and push. "Any moment now," she said, her voice steady. She reached within Tamar, then pulled her hand away and gave her an astonished look.

"This is not one child," she said. "You are carrying two."

All the rollicking and constant kicking within her over the past few months suddenly made sense to Tamar. Two warred within, whereas she had thought her growing child had the arms and feet of a centipede.

Tamar felt the stabbing pain of an overwhelming contraction.

"Here it is!" the midwife exclaimed.

It? He? She?

She watched as the midwife grabbed a scarlet thread from her things. "This one came out first," she said. "I tied the scarlet thread around his wrist to be sure."

His?

The midwife gasped as Tamar felt her stomach tumble over on itself. *What is happening?*

Tamar bit down hard on a stick amid her pain. Blood trickled from the corner of her cheek. "What is it?" she managed to choke out.

The midwife maneuvered into a new position. "What! How did you break out first?" She pulled a squalling baby from Tamar's half-empty womb.

She lay the newborn baby, still bloody, into Tamar's open arms.

"Perez," Tamar said with a laugh to the determined baby who had broken out first. She had little time to count his toes or gaze into his earth-brown eyes before the midwife urged her to push again. Tamar pulled in a breath, then exhaled as a scream and a heave. Another cry slipped into the world, strong and insistent. While the midwife's helper swaddled baby Perez, the midwife placed Tamar's second son upon her breast.

"I will name you Zerah," she said, "the boy with the scarlet bracelet."

The Biblical Narrative

The story of Tamar of Judah is found bracketed in the middle of the story of Joseph in Genesis 38. At first it appears to be a strange interruption to the larger arc, and yet, if you look at the two stories with a critical eye, you see they make different choices under similar circumstances. Tamar's father-in-law Judah is Joseph's older brother—and both were facing various trials. Consider these facts:

Judah	Joseph
Prospers	Causes Potiphar to prosper
Solicits a prostitute	Rebuffs an immoral woman who tries to seduce him
Leaves his seal, cord, and staff with "the prostitute"	Leaves his cloak in the immoral woman's hand as he flees from her
Falsely judges Tamar	Is falsely judged by Potiphar
Produces heirs, saving Israel's line	Preserves the entire nation of Israel

I've often heard Tamar of Judah interpreted scandalously in sermons as someone who used her feminine wiles to secure a place in the family lineage. But a plain reading of Scripture forces us to bump into Judah's very own words: "She is more righteous than I am." He could have said something like, "We both were in the wrong, but my wrong was worse than her wrong." But instead, he tells the reader that Tamar is "righteous." Why is this?

Tamar of Judah, as hinted in the story you just read, had a high view of the things of God. She knew the covenantal nature of the one who promised Father Abraham innumerable offspring. From one seed—Isaac, the chosen son—would come an entire nation-state (Israel), and that people would woo the entire world toward their God because through them would come the Messiah. God's heart for the entire world is wrapped up in the words he spoke to Abraham:

> "Leave your native country, your relatives, and your father's family, and go to the land that I will show you. I will make you into a great nation. I will bless you and make you famous, and you will be a blessing to others. I will bless those who bless you and curse those who treat you with contempt. All the families of the earth will be blessed through you." (Genesis 12:1–3)

These words must've echoed through Tamar's mind, because she was zealous to ensure offspring for the most prominent of the twelve tribes of Israel.

This was no small desire; as you read through the entirety of the Bible, you will see that Tamar's outrageous plan resulted in twins who became forefathers of King David and King Jesus.

But how, exactly, was Tamar forgotten?

First, she is a Canaanite woman—an outsider by definition within her Israelite clan. She is the descendent of Noah's son Ham, who looked on his father's nakedness (See Genesis 9:22–25). Generations before she came along, when Isaac reached the age of marriage and his parents began to search for a potential wife, Abraham ensured that his servant would find a woman from among his own people, outside the heathen Canaanite culture.

Second, in the patriarchal culture of the Old Testament, women thrived economically through marriage and having children. They relied on men to keep them safe and provide for their needs; as with many cultures since then, a woman's value was based on her fecundity. Since Tamar had been widowed twice and had no children to carry on the line of Judah, her only recourse was to follow his advice and return to her family.

To further understand Tamar's desperate situation, we must look at the Levirate Law Moses implemented to keep family lines continuing. Tamar could not simply search for a new husband from another family; she had to wait. In Deuteronomy 25:5–6, Moses wrote,

> If two brothers are living together on the same property and one of them dies without a son, his widow may not be married to anyone from outside the family. Instead, her husband's brother should marry her and have intercourse with her to fulfill the duties of a brother-in-law. The first son she bears to him will be considered the son of the dead brother, so that his name will not be forgotten in Israel.

In giving Onan to Tamar as her husband, Judah was fulfilling this law.

Verse 9 provides a loophole to this, though it's not positive: If the brother refuses his duty,

> the widow must walk over to him in the presence of the elders, pull his sandal from his foot, and spit in his face. Then she must declare, "This is what happens to a man who refuses to provide his brother with children."

Not only that, but the one who refuses is in danger of ridicule. Verse

10 tells us: "Ever afterward in Israel his family will be referred to as 'the family of the man whose sandal was pulled off.'"

Even though Onan obeyed Judah and married Tamar, he did not fulfill his duties to produce an heir for his brother. This angered God, and Onan died.

So Tamar was forced to wait for Shelah, the third son, to marry her if she wished to produce an heir.

Whether Judah worried that Shelah was evil and would die because of his own wrongdoing (as his first two sons did) or believed that Tamar was evil and somehow cursed her husbands, he still made a deliberate choice not to obey the Levirate Law the second time. Not only that, but he transgressed the law by hiring a prostitute after his wife died.

How Does This Apply to Forgotten You?

What does Tamar's experience mean for us? We do not live under Levirate Law, and I'm grateful for that. I do not want to marry my husband's brother. In our postmodern society, women do not need marriage or children to live fully and with provision. We can pay our bills through employment. But there are many ways we might feel similarly overlooked, particularly when someone breaks a monetary promise:

- When someone swindles or cons us
- When someone harms us physically or emotionally, then moves on—leaving us to wrestle through the aftermath alone
- When someone marginalizes a group to which we belong

I felt compelled to address this last question, so I asked my followers on Twitter, "When have you felt overlooked at church?" A flood of responses came back, particularly around two demographics: singles and those middle-aged and older.

- "I'm not the most charismatic speaker, and I don't fit the image of the picture-perfect churchgoer. Thus, I'm constantly overlooked."
- "Last weekend I visited a church where there was literally no small group available to me. [I did not] fit the criteria for any of their life groups."
- "As a forty-five-year-old, never-married single woman, I don't fit into young adult or singles groups. On Sunday mornings, when we do our prayer moment, we're told to pray with those we came with. But I come alone."
- "Most women's ministry events are themed on being a good wife or mother. I'm neither."
- "As we get older and less able to serve, staff are less inclined to talk to us."
- "Having it pointed out that I didn't know what I was talking about because I didn't have kids was the last straw. Something did break in me that has never been repaired."
- "In one of the liturgical prayers for the people, the prayers focus on meeting married people's needs, but the prayer for single people is that they 'be a blessing to others.' Single people apparently don't have needs worth praying about."
- "Church is not a safe place for single people (by that I mean people still single over the typical marriageable age.)"
- "When sharing frustration with a church leader, I was told I was 'ministry middle-aged.' I was too old to be relevant and too young to be considered sage."
- "I'm divorced and often feel like I don't fit. I had to choose

> to fit myself where I felt best fed and let others work it out for themselves."

If any of these statements reflect your experience, I'm so sorry. I wish that all people in the Body of Christ knew their worth, that each leader would recognize the priesthood of all believers and this truth: "A spiritual gift is given to each of us so we can help each other" (1 Corinthians 12:7). Friend, you are made in the image of God. He has endowed you with gifts to serve. Being prevented from exercising those gifts can cause great grief.

The word that comes to mind here is *gatekeeper*. Just as Judah kept the gate of Tamar's ability to flourish and thrive, we sometimes experience being overlooked by gatekeepers who can thwart the fulfillment of our desires and needs. Of course, one way to work through this is to ask, *How would I like to be noticed?* We can take our pain of being overlooked to Jesus and ask him to please help us *not* do that to others. We can allow our pain to be our catalyst for change through the power of the Holy Spirit.

But once we've done that, we can learn much from what Tamar did during a desperate season of overlooking.

First, she never once cursed God for her lot. She did not complain. No doubt she grieved, wore the clothing of widowhood, and agonized over her limbo state, but she did not blame the God of Israel for it. Perhaps she understood that God was a faithful, covenantal God. She endured.

She thought through what she might do. Hers was not a reactionary response, but a calculated one, possibly fueled by her aging body (after all, she would not be fertile forever). So she became proactive. In her mind, the only way to carry on the family line of her late husband Er was to circumvent the promise of Shelah (which seemed empty) by going to the family's primary source—Judah.

Tamar also thought well into her future. She anticipated that her possible pregnancy would incur her father-in-law's judgment, so she requested items that would identify him as the father of her child. His signet was a seal made of stone, engraved with a sigil, which he used to seal and sign important documents. The cord—probably attached to keep the seal from getting lost—could've been a tassel, and it may have been worn as a belt, necklace, or bracelet.[1] Judah's staff itself symbolized his status.

> The signet, cord, and staff represent the emblems of the individual's personal status—much like an ancient identity card. The fact that Judah possessed a signet, dressed in a garment decorated with tassels or wore his signet with a cord as jewelry, and had a staff in hand attests to his high status and importance as a leader.[2]

Imagine the moxie it must've taken Tamar to challenge someone of Judah's status, particularly since she was a foreigner! Literary critic Harold Bloom writes,

> She is single-minded, fearless, and totally self-confident, and she has absolute insight into Judah. Most crucially, she knows that she *is* the future, and she sets aside societal and male-imposed conventions to arrive at her truth, which will turn out to be Yahweh's truth, or David. Her sons are born without stigma, and she too is beyond stigma.[3]

In addition, Tamar does not panic. This part of the story particularly resonates with me. When I'm overlooked, and especially when I feel like I'm being judged unfairly, my first response is to panic—and when I panic, I tend to make very poor choices, including sinful ones. Instead, Tamar calmly addresses the men who are there to arrest her. She reveals the three items that identify the baby's father, and then waits for all to be made right—which ends up happening.

It's important to remember that Judah himself calls Tamar righteous. He does not fault her, but instead honors her by allowing her twin sons to take their rightful place in the family. And he never sleeps with her again.

Tamar's dedication was primarily to the covenantal God who does understand, who notices the broken, and who sees those cast aside as widows. Throughout the Old Testament, we see God's heart for what scholars call "The Quartet of the Vulnerable" (widows, orphans, alien, poor). She embodied three of those states, and possibly all four.

For those of us who are overlooked in church, as well as facing unseen-ness in other areas of our lives, a glance forward toward the book of Hebrews may encourage us. "Patient endurance is what you need now, so that you will continue to do God's will. Then you will receive all that he has promised" (10:26). What an encouraging promise!

Truths about Unforgotten You

- Even when those in power overlook you, God takes note of you.
- It's not wrong to think through a strategic response to receive justice in a painful situation.
- It's OK to name and mourn what you've walked through.
- God blesses your obedience.
- God's character can be trusted even when people's cannot.

Questions for Discussion

1. What did you initially believe about Tamar of Judah before you picked up this book?
2. Why do you think people are quick to judge her?
3. What do you admire about Tamar now that you've looked at her story more closely?
4. When have you experienced being overlooked at church? On your job? In your family?
5. What cultural changes have taken place since Tamar's life? What has remained the same?

CHAPTER TWO

Miriam, the Unsung One

Heart pounding, lungs screaming, young Miriam fought to keep pace with the rapids of the Nile. The cries of her mother, Jochebed, and the soothing words of her father, Amram, echoed through her mind as her wee brother Moses floated in a little tar-pitched basket in the waves. She flanked him along the wide river's bank, stumbling over the shallows of the shoreline, careful to avoid sharp rocks and sticks. *Don't cry. Don't cry.*

She said this to both herself and to him, knowing the precariousness of their situation. She, a Hebrew slave, knew to be quiet and unobtrusive, but Moses understood nothing other than the fact that he was hungry. He began to whimper as his floating cradle left the protection of Goshen and headed toward the realm of Egyptian royalty.

Panicked, Miriam tried, unsuccessfully, to hush-sing to the beautiful baby from her place in the rushes, to calm his fears and somehow sate his stomach's screams. The sharp weeds cut at her calves, but still she sang the lullaby. Singing soothed her, reminding her of Yahweh's faithfulness.

Unlulled, Moses let out a wail just as a princess of Egypt bathed. The beautiful woman noticed the little yelping package and untangled the basket from the reeds.

Miriam crouched behind a particularly tall stand of cattails, holding her breath. What would happen? Would Moses be killed like all the other Hebrew boys had been? It had been the princess's father, the Pharoah of all the land, who had decreed such an abomination. Miriam prayed, asking God for protection, for favor, but really all she knew to say was *help*.

At that moment, the day that had been humid and cloudy became sunlit. A shaft of light seemed to shine on Moses and the princess. She picked him up, cooing to him and clucking rhythmically. "This must be one of the Hebrew children," she told her attendants.

At that moment, Miriam felt the familiar nudge of the Almighty. *Go to her.*

Letting out the breath she held, Miriam kept her eyes low, toward the grass on the mighty Nile's banks. And then she looked up, caught the gaze of the princess, and dared to speak. "Should I go and find one of the Hebrew women to nurse the baby for you?" she asked.

"Yes, do!"

Miriam ran home to find Jochebed tear-stained and red-faced. "Come quickly, Mama," Miriam said.

But Mama would not move.

"Moses is alive!" Miriam explained in a rush. "The Pharaoh's daughter has taken pity on him, and now he needs a wet nurse. Come!"

She led her along the riverbank back to the princess, whose eyes wept with relief.

"Take this baby and nurse him for me," she said to Jochebed. "I will pay you for your help."

Those halcyon days of nursing and nurturing brought joy to them all. Moses would live, and their family would have the rare opportunity to pour into him before he had to return full time to the palace. Miriam taught Moses the songs of their people. Big brother Aaron encouraged Moses to crawl, then walk. Mama and Papa danced with the young baby, then toddler, to the rhythm of Yahweh's ways. And through it all, they cried quietly at night, begging Yahweh for deliverance from oppression. Slavery stole any freedom, and it would abscond with Moses in due time.

On the day of surrender, Mama brought Moses to Pharoah's home. The family's grief on that day was tangible. For a long time, no one spoke over the evening meal. It was the quiet that settled in on them all. No toddler laughter. No songs of their people. No sweet-smelling skin or bright eyes. Just silence.

Miriam missed Moses, often wondering what he was experiencing. Though her other brother, Aaron, was nearby, she constantly worried about their little one. At least she knew that in Pharaoh's palace, he was protected from the backbreaking labor they all endured as slaves.

In the rumblings of her heart, Miriam knew a divine secret. For several years, she had seen pinprick glimpses of what the future held. Mama called these inklings the gift of "prophecy," and told her it was important to steward her gift with humility. The one consistent word she felt in her gut was this: Moses would deliver their nation from slavery. The one whose name meant "drawing out," who himself had been drawn from the Nile, would set their people free from the tyranny of the Egyptians.

But Miriam dared not proclaim such a thing in public. She kept it hidden as a delightful and perplexing secret, waiting for the moment when Moses would take a stand.

She thought that prophetic moment arrived late one afternoon when the sun began its rapid descent in the west. Though she did not witness Moses's actions, she heard the story repeated in hushed tones throughout the camp.

An Egyptian beating one of their countrymen. Moses's indignation and wrath. His muscled torso ripping into the Egyptian, snuffing out his life, then burying his body in the sand. And then what happened the next day when he saw an Israelite fighting a fellow Israelite. "Why are you beating up your friend?" he had asked. The retort about everyone knowing he had murdered an Egyptian.

Moses's exclamation, "Everyone knows what I did."

Pharoah seeking the death penalty for Moses—and Moses fleeing to save his own life. But this time, Miriam could not follow as his protector. Her ache over his absence grew as tall as the pyramids, and with it, doubt. Had she heard from God correctly? Was Moses's power to deliver his people limited to killing one Egyptian and nothing else?

Forty years passed—so much life contained in four decades of loss and slavery and groaning.

But at the end of that time, Miriam held her brother Moses again—clung to him, actually. His self-imposed exile had been broken by the Lord.

Moses told her of his commissioning from the mouth of an unconsumed yet burning shrub.

"What of your speech?" she asked him as they walked through the encampment.

His attempt to respond melted into stutters. Finally, he coughed out, "Aaron will be my mouthpiece. And, and, God will show his powers." He threw his staff to the ground, and she watched as it became a slithering serpent, then morphed back into his rigid staff when he picked it up by the tail.

Perhaps he will be our deliverer! Miriam cherished this thought in her heart, realizing that God had shown her the future—but the way he would work out those promises might be slow, arduous, and, yet, perfect in timing.

Miriam watched as her brothers confronted the most powerful god-man in the land: Pharoah himself. Their mantra? Yahweh's words: "Let My people go so they may hold a festival in My honor in the wilderness." But Pharoah, she learned, would have none of that. He deepened the Israelites' pain by calling them lazy and forcing them to make bricks without straw. She fought to encourage her countrymen to have faith, to believe that God would deliver them—but grumbling had become their native language in the land of exile and pain.

The fickle Pharaoh teased often, saying yes, the people could go, then reneging even through a cataclysmic series of God's judgments: bloody water, leaping frogs, itching lice, pestering flies, sickened livestock, festering boils, boulder-sized hail, gnawing locusts, then crippling darkness. But the final judgment—the death of the firstborn—dealt a decisive blow. God said through Moses and Aaron that he would make a distinction between the people of Israel and the people of Egypt, but only blood would create the dichotomy.

The Israelite families each butchered an entire lamb, one without blemish. They drained its blood into an awaiting basin. As instructed, they dipped hyssop branches into the blood, then painted it on the tops and sides of their doorframes until the blood raced earthward like veins. The smell of warm blood sickened her, but she knew enough about the God of her people that when he instructed them to stay within their homes that night, they would be foolish to disobey.

At midnight the roar of distant cries began—the wailing of mothers, the hee-hawing of donkeys, the rage of fathers. The Lord God Almighty had kept his promise to judge the nation that enslaved his chosen people—yet no one in the Israelite encampment suffered grief that night.

At dawn, Miriam and all the other women did as God had instructed, asking for treasure from the Egyptians before they hastened away from their land of enslavement. At Succoth, she looked back briefly, wondering if her gaze would earn her the same fate as Lot's wife. It didn't.

The Israelites did not venture in the obvious direction, though—the one that would take them through Philistine territory—the shortest route toward their Promised Land. Instead, God led them circuitously toward the banks of the Sea of Reeds, leading the way as a pillar of cloud by day and fire by night. They walked through Ethan, then pitched camp at Pi-hahiroth between Migdol and the imposing sea, just across from Baal-zephon.

Only after they settled there did Miriam spot the mighty army of Egypt, with its dust-churning chariots pounding the earth. Cries of "Why did you bring us out here to die in the wilderness?" "Weren't there enough graves for us in Egypt?" "What have you done to us?" and "Why did you make us leave Egypt?" punctuated the camp. She marveled at her brother's ability to face the criticism without fear. Still, the words were relentless:

"Didn't we tell you this would happen while we were still in Egypt?" *Well, actually, no.*

"We said, 'Leave us alone! Let us be slaves to the Egyptians.'"

Do you understand what you're saying? Have you already forgotten the shackles of slavery we've endured?

"It's better to be a slave in Egypt than a corpse in the wilderness!" *Is it? Does not freedom beat a song of victory in your heart?*

But Miriam, a woman gifted with a prophetic voice, stayed mute. Instead, she marveled at his words to the nation.

"Don't be afraid," he said. "Just stand still and watch the Lord rescue you today. The Egyptians you see today will never be seen again. The Lord will himself fight for you. Just stay calm." Moses's words of gutsy faith enflamed her as she watched her little brother (now a man!) directing her people toward the mighty Sea. The pillar of fire flanked them, providing a temporary shield from the approaching army.

Then the miracle happened.

Moses raised his hand skyward, waving it over the churning waters of chaos beneath. At that moment, a furious wind began to blow from the east. It battered tents and people alike, making it impossible for Miriam to keep her head covering from releasing her hair into the night air. And as her long hair tangled, the Sea receded. She watched as it stacked itself up itself on the north and south, leaving a pathway through its belly.

With Moses leading the way, all six million Israelites walked that path, marveling at the stands of wind-walled water around them. The Lord Almighty had created a way of refuge, proving to the nation that he was a covenantal God who powerfully kept his promises of deliverance.

Once across, though, Miriam worried. The army of Egypt, once an impossible giant in her eyes, did not stop at the sea's edge. No, they kept plowing toward them, churning their way through the footprints their former slaves had left behind. Miriam prayed, then prayed some more. *Please, God. See us here. Take notice.*

Yahweh noticed. He twisted chariot wheels with the strength of his unseen hand.

From the middle of the path, Miriam heard a general shout: "Let's get out of here—away from these Israelites! The LORD is fighting for them against Egypt." Panic laced the words.

Moses raised his hand over the impossible Sea.

The angry, salted sea swallowed the cries of the Egyptians in a flash. Wheels and chariots and horses tumbled in a boiling cauldron of God's judgment.

Then calm. No horses. No chariots. No army. No Pharoah.

The only response was a song. Moses, who suddenly found his voice in the aftermath of God's great deliverance, sang of his warrior ways, his mighty acts of punishing the wicked, the power of his arm to save, and the ability of his right hand to smash their enemy. He sang of God's great majesty and the futility of rising against him. Miriam joined the chorus, elevating God's holiness, wonder, splendor, love, leadership, might, and sovereignty. She sang and sang and sang worship to the God of deliverance.

And then, she heard God's voice. He gave her a simple song of her own.

Sing to the Lord,
For he has triumphed gloriously;
He has hurled both horse and rider into the sea.

This she taught to the women of Israel, a tambourine as her instrument. They joined the chorus with the jangle of tambourine and the shuffling of dancing feet. This moment, she knew, must be celebrated. The triumph of God deserved unashamed dancing. She thanked him for the words, the melody, and the celebration that ensued.

But the years of circling the wilderness wore on Miriam. She and her brothers had weathered the people's mockery, their longing to return to slavery, God's judgment against them for the horrific episode with the golden calf—led by Aaron, and the grumbling that had become more the national rule than the exception.

At Hazeroth, Miriam conferred with Aaron over the ethnicity of Moses's new wife. Why did he marry a Cushite? Why not marry within the tribe? Didn't God specifically speak only to their people? Wouldn't Moses's new wife bend his heart away from the best interests of the nation? Would she have undue influence on him? And what of *their* influence? Hadn't God spoken to them as well? Why would God only choose one fallible man to lead his people—a man prone to marrying foreign wives, at that?

Together, they confronted Moses in his tent. Miriam spoke first. "Hasn't the Lord spoken through us, too?" Before she could say another word, God himself summoned them to the Tabernacle, its doorway flapping open in the hot desert breeze. His resonant, earth-shaking voice reverberated through her, shaking her bones, and rattling her vocal cords.

"If there were prophets among you, I, the Lord, would reveal myself in visions," he said. "I would speak to them in dreams. But not with my servant Moses. Of all my house, he is the one I trust. I speak to him face to face, clearly, and not in riddles! He sees the Lord as he is. So why were you not afraid to criticize my servant, Moses?"

Miriam looked over at Aaron, whose countenance turned blue. The cloud shifted from above the tabernacle, allowing the sun to spotlight her. And in that holy gaze of light, her skin whitened with leprosy.

It was Aaron who interceded, though his voice sounded small and panicked. "Oh, my master! Please don't punish us for this sin we have so foolishly committed," he said. "Don't let her be like a stillborn baby, already decayed at birth."

Moses, the one who saw God as a friend, fell facedown. "O God, I beg you, please heal her!"

The Lord answered from the distancing cloud, "If her father had done nothing more than spit in her face, wouldn't she be defiled for seven days? So keep her outside the camp for seven days, and after that she may be accepted back."

When they exiled Miriam to the outer camp, she welcomed it as a relief. She deserved such a judgment. She had valued her own voice, and the timing of her proclamations over patience in waiting for God to act. She had despised God's appointed leader. Those seven days she spent keeping herself away from flames, or cold or sharp edges, as she lost feeling in her extremities and could not trust herself to prevent injury. But a week later, God healed her—and restored her to her people, to Aaron, to Moses.

And she thanked him.

The Biblical Narrative

Miriam, whose name means "bitter," played an important role in the life of Moses and the freeing of Israel. We find her story throughout the book of Exodus, primarily in Exodus 2 and 5. We see her leprous rebellion in Numbers 12. She is one of eight prophetesses mentioned in the Old and New Testaments. The minor prophet Micah credits Miriam when he writes, "For I brought you out of Egypt and redeemed you from slavery. I sent Moses, Aaron, and Miriam to help you" (Micah 6:4). The story of her leprosy seems to have been spurred by a moment of jealousy over Moses's connection to God and leadership position—stemming from a sense of feeling overlooked.

Her overlookedness is nuanced, something we see only as we look at her entire story. It's easy to feel overlooked or under-seen in a moment, not realizing how our responses to it in the day-to-day effect eternity. Think about it: Had Miriam not chased after Moses's basket in the Nile as a child, would he have been rescued? Perhaps—but would her mother have known of it? Would Moses be lost to history, serving out the rest of his days as a son of the mighty Pharoah? He must've known something about his people from their people's perspective since he sought to free them. Who could've told him those stories but Miriam or Aaron, or maybe their parents, while he was being nursed? Certainly, Pharoah would not have taught Moses to have empathy for the enslaved nation.

There is also aloneness in having a rare or unusual gift. The Bible names approximately one hundred male prophets, compared to only eight women who held that office. Can you relate? Have you ever felt overlooked in your gifting? Have you felt sidelined or unimportant in the ministry structure the modern church has embraced?

How This Applies to Unsung You

What can we learn from Miriam when we walk through the pain of being overlooked? How can her faithfulness encourage our own?

Miriam battled for the unsung.

In watching over Moses, she risked death (as a child!) to keep him safe. In other words, she cared less about her own status than about her brother's survival. She reminds us of the important truth Jesus told his disciples in the upper room before his crucifixion: "For even the Son of Man came not to be served but to serve others and to give his life as a ransom for many" (Mark 10:45).

When we're constantly seeking to be served and thinking of our own interests, we lose sight of the greater joy of serving others. We grow in Christ not by seeking the limelight, but by humbly protecting those within our sphere of influence.

Miriam exercised her gifts, come what may.

Like every human being, Miriam was endowed with gifts from her Creator. And she exercised them, declaring the greatness of God after a miraculous victory through the Red Sea. She didn't ask for permission to speak; she just spoke. She didn't shrink from her calling; she stepped boldly into it.

We see prophetic giftings throughout the Bible. According to Pastor Mike Signorelli,

> prophecy is simply the mind of God migrating into the mind of humanity. Prophecy is one way that God's thoughts and ways are communicated to us today. It can sometimes look like encouragement, and sometimes it can look like foretelling of the future.[1]

After Jesus lived the perfect life, died in place of sinful humanity, and rose again, the church was born. With that, God gave all his people gifts. The Apostle Peter puts it this way:

> God has given each of you a gift from his great variety of spiritual gifts. Use them well to serve one another. Do you have the gift of speaking? Then speak as though God himself were speaking through you. Do you have the gift of helping others? Do it with all the strength and energy that God supplies. Then everything you do will bring glory to God through Jesus Christ. (1 Peter 4:10–11)

Here, Peter reminds us that God has empowered us to use the gifts he's given us. So often in the gospels, we see Jesus telling various parables about doing our best with what we've been given, to be faithful in small things so we can be entrusted with much. Miriam chose to do that.

The Apostle Paul takes for granted the fact that women can be prophetic when he writes in 1 Corinthians 11:5, "But a woman dishonors her head if she prays or prophesies without a covering on her head, for this is the same as shaving her head." Modern readers can get easily stuck in the controversy of head coverings yet miss the profound point that women can and do exercise their prophetic gifts within their congregations.

Sadly, women are often overlooked in ministry contexts, but that is no excuse to give up or shrink back. As we will see with many of these overlooked women, they did not allow their unseen status to deter them from carrying out the work of God. We always have a choice to do so, even if we are afraid of what others may think or how harshly they may judge us.

Miriam was faithful over a lifetime.

No human being is perfect, and as we saw with Miriam's insubordination and consequent leprosy, nevertheless, she repented. After being welcomed back into the commonwealth of Israel, she lived out her days. We learn in Numbers 20:1 of her fate:

> In the first month of the year, the whole community of Israel arrived in the wilderness of Zin and camped at Kadesh. While they were there, Miriam died and was buried.

Like Moses, Miriam was not allowed to enter the Promised Land. Even so, we honor her for her important role in helping bring the

Israelites freedom from slavery. You, too, are tasked with faithfulness throughout your lifetime, to finish the race before you with vigor and faith.

Miriam's shortcomings teach an important lesson about grumbling.

As mentioned above, Miriam was like the rest of us. She got discouraged. She may have been jealous of Moses's status or his ability to connect deeply with his Creator. And we see from the fictionalized account above that she and Aaron both grumbled about Moses's selection of a second mate from Cush. The result? Leprosy and a weeklong banishment from camp. Earlier, Moses had reprimanded the entire nation for a similar act when the people complained about the food God was providing in the wilderness.

> Then Moses added, "The Lord will give you meat to eat in the evening and bread to satisfy you in the morning, for he has heard all your complaints against him. What have we done? Yes, your complaints are against the Lord, not against us." (Exodus 16:8)

Grumbling and complaining make us incapable of seeing God's goodness. They tarnish our ability to have faith in His provision. So often throughout the Old Testament, Israel's sin was the act of complaining and giving in to their fear. The Psalmist puts it plainly: "Instead, they grumbled in their tents and refused to obey the Lord" (Psalm 106:25). See the connection between grumbling and disobedience here? They seem to operate in tandem and give rise to malcontent. When we are overlooked, our first response is often to complain, and the longer we stay in that bitter cycle, the less apt we are to thank God for His provision and kindness. Paul found this so important that he told the Philippian believers, "Do everything without complaining and arguing" (Philippians 2:14).

When God brought victory, Miriam celebrated.

In fact, she penned a victory song, then led her countrywomen in worship with tambourines and dancing. She embodied Psalm 145:4, which says: "Let each generation tell its children of your mighty acts; let them proclaim your power."

What would happen if, when we feel overlooked, we sought to find the victory God has brought our way and then, counterintuitively, worshiped him for all he has done for us? Look at all the ways the psalmist praises God in Psalm 150 and note that Miriam embodied several of these after the Israelites crossed through the Red Sea unharmed:

> Praise the Lord!
> Praise God in his sanctuary;
> praise him in his mighty heaven!
> Praise him for his mighty works;
> praise his unequaled greatness!
> Praise him with a blast of the ram's horn;
> praise him with the lyre and harp!
> Praise him with the tambourine and dancing;
> praise him with strings and flutes!
> Praise him with a clash of cymbals;
> praise him with loud clanging cymbals.
> Let everything that breathes sing praises to the Lord!
> Praise the Lord!

God disciplined Miriam for her own good.

When Miriam felt overlooked, then gave full vent to her frustration, God disciplined her. Why? Because he wanted the best for her and helping her get it required helping her to change her perspective. In the book of Job, we see a man who also is righteous in God's eyes yet is still disciplined. At the beginning of the book, Job hears God, but after his excessive trial, Job *sees* God. Discipline from God was the bridge between merely hearing and seeing God.

> "But consider the joy of those corrected by God! Do not despise the discipline of the Almighty when you sin. For though he wounds, he also bandages. He strikes, but his hands also heal." (Job 5:17–18)

This is certainly not a popular topic in today's Christian circles, which are bent more toward getting blessings than walking through trials. But if you look back over your life, isn't it true that you learned more from your failures and God's discipline than you learned through your glorious victories?

We learn from the author of Hebrews about the powerful benefits of God's sweet discipline.

> For our earthly fathers disciplined us for a few years, doing the best they knew how. But God's discipline is always good for us, so that we might share in his holiness. No discipline is enjoyable while it is happening—it's painful! But afterward there will be a peaceful harvest of right living for those who are trained in this way. (Hebrews 12:10–11)

Whether we are overlooked or not, welcoming God's discipline is part of our sanctification journey. It reveals God's love for us, that he loves us so much that he wants our hearts to grow and flourish and exercise more and more faith.

As followers of Christ, we are called not only to heed God's discipline, but to cultivate discipline within ourselves. One of the fruits of the Spirit, after all, is self-control. The Apostle Paul puts it this way, using athletic metaphors:

> I discipline my body like an athlete, training it to do what it should. Otherwise, I fear that after preaching to others I myself might be disqualified. (1 Corinthians 9:27)

Discipline is both reaction (how we respond to God's correction) and proaction (how we choose to exercise self-control throughout our lives). It's a normative process in the Christian life because, even though our sins are forgiven, we still battle with the tendency to grumble and stumble.

Miriam reminds us that part of the human condition is to be overlooked at times, but we can still find meaning and joy in using our God-given gifts for His glory. We can persevere for years, even when our lives feel like an overly long wilderness journey. We can learn to practice gratitude and contentment. And we can spend our lives serving others, even rescuing the helpless and partnering with God to emancipate them.

Truths about Celebrated You

- The Kingdom of God consists of small actions that have an unseen but huge impact.
- When God brings victory in your life, sing.

- Grumbling can cost you.
- God disciplines those he loves.

Questions for Discussion

1. How much did you know about the life of Miriam before reading this book?
2. How does her protection of baby Moses inspire you?
3. Recall a time in your life that God did something amazing and you chose to celebrate. Conversely, can you remember a time when you neglected worship after a breakthrough?
4. Why do you think the world praises the outward ministries that are in the spotlight? What does Miriam's story teach you about unseen obedience?
5. What does the story of Miriam's leprosy teach you about God's character?

CHAPTER THREE

Zelophehad's Daughters, the Unnoticed Ones

The plague ravaged the land, destroyed families, and made life in its aftermath a wincing affair. Mahlah comforted her sisters Noah, Hoglah, Milcah, and Tirzah. "All will be well, sisters," she said in the confines of their tent. "We have been counted, and since we were counted, perhaps we will inherit also."

But Noah, headstrong and with fiery eyes, cleared her throat. "Counting means nothing. Our father had no sons. Therefore, we will be destitute." She paced the tent, wringing her hands.

"Surely there has to be a way," young Tirzah said. "Our family has overcome so much—slavery, the sea, instability, the plague—"

"It means nothing," Milcah cried. "It's as if they have no recollection of our lineage." At this, Milcah joined Noah's pacing. "Ours is the heritage of Joseph. The one who preserved our nation and protected us all from annihilation by famine. Ours is a royal line."

Mahlah shushed her. "It matters not that Joseph begat Manasseh, begat Makir, begat Giliad, begat Hepher, begat our father, Zelophehad. That was over a century ago. Memories, though important, don't protect us today." Mahlah's tears came then, furiously, as if they'd been held in by a very weak dam. "We will be cast out and starved to death."

Hoglah, usually meek and silent, stood and embraced Mahlah. "Sister, dear sister," she soothed. "This is no time to give up hope. We must remember the kindness of our God, the one who takes notice of the outcast, the alien, the orphan, the widow. He loves and cares for those people, so why won't he take care of us?"

"With Father dead," Milcah said, "we *are* orphaned."

Hers was a statement of logic, Mahlah knew, but it brought her small comfort. Mahlah wiped away her tears with her *palla* and told herself to think back to the faithfulness of God. "Hoglah's right. We need to remember the *hesed* of our God. Through all these years of following fire and cloud, God has been our shelter, our provider, our constant one. We have not yet starved. We have survived the plague. We have been counted in the census." She paced the tent once again, but this time her mind whirred with the remembrance of God's faithful, covenantal love.

Little Tirzah, both because she was the youngest and because of her small stature, got on her knees in the sand. The other sisters followed.

"God in heaven, Savior of Israel, giver of fire and cloud, defender of orphans and widows, hear our prayer," Tirzah said. "We are your daughters, and we are in need. Please show us what to do. We do not want to overstep our position. We understand our precarious situation. Please reveal to us how to proceed in a way that honors you and yet preserves our lives. Look on us with favor. I dare to even ask that we would be allotted our share of the land due to our father. Please help us, Almighty God."

They continued to kneel in silence, waiting. Suddenly an idea, clear as the Nile River before its yearly flood, burst into Mahlah's mind. Dare she? Could she? Could they if they made the bold request together? Or should she shrink backward, stay in their tent, and accept their fate?

She shared the idea as they sat in a circle together, eyes wet with tears. Her voice shook as she detailed the plan to stand before Moses himself and make the audacious request.

"We will approach the leader tomorrow," she said.

The next morning, Mahlah, Noah, Hoglah, Milcah, and Tirzah left their tent and headed toward the entrance of the Tabernacle. Mahlah could feel the surprised stares of her people upon them as they made their way through the dusty day to appeal to Moses. Approaching him as a band of sisters would upset the cultural apple cart, at the very least, but it was their only recourse. Mahlah adjusted her head covering and took in a hot, desert breath.

Before her stood Moses, their deliverer, the friend of God, the prophet, the one who had given their people the Commandments. Behind him stood Eleazar the priest, and flanking him were all the tribal leaders. Spreading beyond them were their countrymen—their entire community at the Tabernacle's main entrance.

I can't do this.

Moses nodded Mahlah's way as if to say, *What do you need?* His eyes were authoritative, but not unkind.

"Our father," Mahlah said, "died in the wilderness." Once she said the words, she knew what Moses was thinking. *Had their father been part of the rebellion of Korah when fire consumed so many for their rebellion?* So she added, "He was not among Korah's followers, who rebelled against the LORD; he died because of his own sin. But he had no sons."

Moses held her gaze, but she dropped it. Steadied herself. Her next words must be careful and clear. The wind whipped around them all in that moment, kicking up dust. She pulled her head covering tighter and shielded her eyes from the sand.

"Why should the name of our father disappear from his clan just because he had no sons?" she said, looking up again. "Give us property along with the rest of our relatives."

There. The request had been made. She looked back at her sisters, catching their frightened gazes. Theirs was an entirely unheard-of request, full of boldness and without legal precedent. Still, she felt the gaze of heaven upon her, the covenantal love of their God. Now their fate would rest in his almighty hands.

"I will bring this case before the Lord," Moses told her. "Wait."

When Moses returned from meeting with the Lord of Hosts in the Tabernacle, Mahlah could see a bit of God's glory still emanating from him. What would he say? What would be their fate?

Moses smiled at her, which calmed her stomach. She held the hands of her four sisters, thanking God that this might be good news.

"The Lord has said your claim is legitimate. I will give you a grant of land along with your father's relatives. I'll assign you the property that would have been given to your father."

Mahlah let out the breath she'd been holding. They would be saved! They would not starve! Their father's name would be preserved. She felt like dancing as Miriam had after the deliverance through the Red Sea. This felt no less miraculous to her.

A bit of an uproar erupted around them. She heard cries of, "This is not how we do things!" and for a moment she panicked. Would the people override the word of the Lord? They had rebelled against him before; perhaps they would do so again.

But Moses calmed the grumblers. "This is what the Lord says to the people of Israel!" His voice boomed above the people, and they settled in to hear. "If a man dies and has no son, then give his inheritance to his daughters. And if he has no daughter either, transfer his inheritance to his brothers. If he has no brothers, give his inheritance to his father's brothers. But if his father has no brothers, give his inheritance to the nearest relative in his clan. This is a legal requirement for the people of Israel, a command of our God."

The sisters embraced each other. In their tent, they sang their joy, dancing in circles and raising cups to the kindness of God. They would be safe. Their father's name would remain forever. All would be well.

Later, camped on the plains of Moab across from mighty Jericho, the nation rested on the banks of the Jordan River. They were just on the cusp of crossing over into the Promised Land. The heads of Gilead's clan approached Moses in a manner like the daughters of Zelophehad.

"Sir," the head clansman said, "The LORD instructed you to divide the land by sacred lot among the people of Israel. You were told by the LORD to give the grant of land owned by our brother Zelophehad to his daughters."

Moses nodded, which calmed Mahlah again. Moses remembered the Lord's decree and his pledge!

"But" the leader continued, "if the girls marry men from

another tribe, their grants of land will go with them to the tribe into which they marry. In this way, the total area of our tribal land will be reduced."

Mahlah had long wondered about that scenario, and she strained to hear what her tribesman would say next.

"Then when the Year of Jubilee comes, their portion of land will be added to that of the new tribe, causing it to be lost forever to ours."

Once again, Moses consulted with God in the Tabernacle. Upon his return, he said, "The claim of the men of the tribe of Joseph is legitimate. This is what the LORD commands concerning the daughters of Zelophehad."

Mahlah twisted her fingers.

"Let them marry anyone they like, as long as it is within their own ancestral tribe. None of the territorial land may pass from tribe to tribe, for all the land given to each tribe must remain within the tribe to which it was first allotted."

Again, Mahlah and her sisters rejoiced over the goodness of God in their tent. They determined to marry cousins from their father's side who also belonged to the clan of Manasseh. This would further confirm that their father's name would not be forgotten, and that all the land allotted to him would be preserved.

Mahlah knew the situation well. Joseph had two sons—Ephraim and Manasseh. While all the other sons of Jacob had tribes named after them, Ephraim and Manasseh's descendants were each recognized as half tribes (rather than the full tribe of Joseph). The half tribe of Manasseh claimed their allotment in Gilead and Bashan on the Jordan River's eastern flank. The western side would be given to the clans of Abiezer, Helek, Asriel, Shechem, Hepher, and Shemida—all representatives of the male descendants of Joseph's son Manasseh.

But would the decree of Moses last now that he had passed on to his fathers?

When Mahlah did not hear their family mentioned, she approached Moses's personal assistant, Joshua, and Eleazar the priest. She pulled in a breath, hoping to steady her voice. She knew she should remain confident. Hadn't God promised them land? And had Moses not said so plainly? Surely, the new leaders, particularly Eleazar, would remember those unprecedented words. "The LORD commanded Moses to give us a grant of land along with the men of our tribe," she said.

Without fanfare, Joshua granted them land alongside their uncles—just as God had commanded. It was a wide, beautiful piece of property, full of arbors and vines and flocks of sheep. In that place of security, Mahlah, Noah, Hoglah, Milcah, and Tirzah settled with their families—keeping their father's name and legacy alive.

The Biblical Narrative

This story is drawn from Numbers 26–27, Numbers 36, Joshua 17, and 1 Chronicles 7. With that in mind, it's hard to understand why more sermons aren't preached about these overlooked women who took their complaint to Moses about receiving an inheritance in the Promised Land even before the conquest of Canaan. Without understanding the cultural context of this story, its significance is lost on Western ears.

At that time in Israel's history, all rights, lands, and inheritances went to the firstborn son, as I mentioned earlier. If there was no son, there was no inheritance. Since Zelophehad had no son, his name would be forgotten, and his other descendants and family members would have no property in the Promised Land.

For women to leave their tent and approach a leader without being called was strictly taboo. That Zelophehad's daughters voluntarily left their dwelling to approach the religious and governmental leaders of their nation was nothing short of astonishing. They would've had to have a compelling reason to do so—in this case, their hope to preserve their father's line which would, in turn, preserve their own lives and ways of earning income.

They ventured to the Tabernacle, the sacred tent that held the Ark of the Covenant. This was a holy place, surrounded only by men, including the legendary Moses. It's hard to imagine how out-of-the-box their approach was. It would be like a regular citizen forcing his way through the Secret Service to speak with the president of the United States. And yet they chose to take that risk. They must have known the Law and discerned a loophole that needed to be called out, which reveals their familiarity with the things of God. The Law, though clear, did not take into account special circumstances that could arise, particularly if a man had no sons. They realized the kindness (*hesed*) and justice of God and sought to remind the leaders of their nation that he would want to be fair to them in their circumstances. They also were clear, concise, and argued their case the way a lawyer would argue before a court. In many ways, that is exactly what they did—except that they hadn't been invited to do so beforehand.

It's also interesting to note that Moses himself named these five sisters in the biblical narrative. They are not referred to only as "Zelophehad's daughters" in the same manner as "Lot's wife" or "Noah's wife" had no first names recorded; he refers to them as Mahlah, Noah, Hoglah, Milcah, and Tirzah. A quick survey of their names' meanings provides some interesting information:

- *Mahlah* means "sickness."[1]
- *Noah* means "movement."[2]
- *Hoglah* means "partridge."[3]
- *Milcah* means "queen."[4]
- *Tirzah* means "pleasure" or "beauty."[5]

Together, their names represent a wide spectrum of humanity—both those who are broken and those who are lauded. And yet, Dr. Ronald Allen of Dallas Theological Seminary commends them not only for their gutsiness, but for their piety.

> These were pious women with a sound understanding of the nature of the desert experience and a just claim for their family. Further, they were women of faith. The people were not in the land yet, but these women knew that they would enter it soon. Their claim to Moses is anticipative of the Lord's deliverance of the people from the awful desert to the Land of Promise.[6]

These five women demonstrated a keen trust in God's ability to deliver the Promised Land to the people of Israel—and by bravely taking their concern to Moses, they created a new legal precedent for the nation that clarified the law regarding exceptions to the patriarchal system, including women's rights to possess land. The Lord's response revealed that justice is more important to Him than tradition. We see this heartbeat of God throughout Scripture, but most pointedly in the Gospel of Matthew.

> Jesus replied, "And why do you, by our traditions, violate the direct commandments of God? For instance, God says, 'Honor your father and mother,' and 'Anyone who

> speaks disrespectfully of father or mother must be put to death.' But you say it is all right for people to say to their parents, 'Sorry, I can't help you. For I have vowed to give to God what I would have given to you.' In this way, you say they don't need to honor their parents. *And so you cancel the word of God for the sake of your own tradition.*" (Matthew 15:3–6, emphasis mine)

If we fast-forward through history to the point when Jesus inaugurates his church, we see more echoes of the daughters' act and God's surprising response in their favor: "There is no longer Jew or Gentile, slave or free, male and female. For you are all one in Christ Jesus" (Galatians 3:28).

Zelophehad's daughters' understanding of God's covenantal love toward those who suffer is also highlighted in their story. They understood God's heart toward the widow, the orphan, the alien, and the poor. Consider these scriptures from the Pentateuch:

- Regarding aliens, orphans, and widows: "True justice must be given to foreigners living among you and to orphans, and you must never accept a widow's garment as security for her debt. Always remember that you were slaves in Egypt and that the Lord your God redeemed you from slavery. That is why I have given you this command." (Deuteronomy 24:17–18)
- Regarding the poor: "Give generously to the poor, not grudgingly, for the Lord your God will bless you in everything you do. There will always be some in the land who are poor. That is why I am commanding you to share freely with the poor and with the other Israelites in need." (Deuteronomy 15:10–11)

Considering this understanding, these overlooked women made their bold request. It's important to note that God responded to it not meagerly, but abundantly, as Precept Austin's Numbers 27 commentary highlighted:

> In fact, the response of the Lord went beyond their request. In verse four they requested an *ʾaḥuzzāh* ("landed property"). The response of the Lord was for an *ʾaḥuzzaṯ naḥalāh* ("a hereditary possession of landed property," v.7). The point seems to be that not only would they receive the property, but they could also transfer it to their heirs as well. Thus they share with the sons of other fathers who were deceased. It is as though their father had had sons![7]

How This Applies to Unnoticed You

The daughters of Zelophehad were once overlooked by their nation, but God did not overlook them. He loved his daughters and created a system of justice for them to flourish amid their countrymen. So what does this mean for us today who have felt the sting of injustice and the pain of being overlooked or unseen?

We can study and understand the heart of God.

God's heart is *for* us.

The Old Testament is replete with verses about God's care for his people. The daughters would've known this truth:

> "Now if you will obey me and keep my covenant, you will be my own special treasure from among all the peoples on the earth; for all the earth belongs to me." (Exodus 19:5)

They were included in this verse as God's particular treasure.

Later, long after the daughters walked the earth, David reminds us in the oft-quoted psalm,

> How precious are your thoughts about me, O God. They cannot be numbered! I can't even count them; they outnumber the grains of sand! And when I wake up, you are still with me! (Psalm 139:17–18)

God's thoughts toward us are innumerable. He is able to think of all his children all the time—and his thoughts are kind, not harsh. As someone who's survived multiple traumas, it's taken a long time for me to understand this, and to be honest, I am just barely grasping God's kindness in this area. When we've been harmed or overlooked for most of our childhood, we tend to project that aloneness onto God unfairly. (Have you done this?)

But the truth is greater than our feelings. We may *feel* overlooked. We may *feel* as if God is an angry taskmaster or tsk-tsk-tsks over us, but the verse above pushes completely against this idea. Friend, when you are overlooked by people in your life, the bedrock truth is this: God is still with you. *With* you. Alongside you. Having innumerable thoughts about you—and *all* of them are good.

Jesus reminds us of his care and kindness in Matthew 10:29–31. Above we see God's thoughts toward us are "innumerable," but here we see our value quantified:

> "What is the price of two sparrows—one copper coin? But not a single sparrow can fall to the ground without your Father knowing it. And the very hairs of your head are all numbered. So don't be afraid; you are more valuable to God than a whole flock of sparrows."

Consider this: The God who creates tiny birds takes note of them. So of course he takes note of you. You are not overlooked by him. Every single strand of your hair is numbered (and his thoughts toward you are an infinitely greater number!), which means every worry you carry is annotated. Experiencing and trusting in God's covenantal love will give you the confidence to walk into situations that scare you. The daughters of Zelophehad exercised this confidence only because they knew the heart of their God. It was the foundation upon which they made their audacious request.

The Apostle Paul reminds us of God's heart toward us as well:

> What shall we say about such wonderful things as these? If God is for us, who can ever be against us? Since he did not spare even his own Son but gave him up for us all, won't he also give us everything else? Who dares accuse us whom God has chosen for his own? No one—for God himself has given us right standing with himself. (Romans 8:31–33)

The "if" in that verse is better rendered as "since." There is no "if": God *is* for us, without question and in every situation. Do you have a hard time grasping that truth? (I do.) But the Bible tells us his heart is bent toward our cries. He loves us. He sent his Son to die on our behalf. He has given us the gift of his Holy Spirit so that we will never be alone. Friend, God is *for* you. He sees you. His heart bends towards you.

We can have faith that sees beyond our season of being overlooked.

Like the author of Hebrews and the daughters of Zelophehad, God can give us the ability to see through lenses of his love for us, which will inform our faith. "Faith" is rendered *pistis* in the Greek. It is the "conviction of the truth of anything, belief . . . the conviction that God exists and is the creator and ruler of all things, the provider and bestower of eternal salvation through Christ . . . *the character of one who can be relied on*" (emphasis mine).[8] Yes, having faith in Jesus is the foundation of our salvation, but that faith is strong because the character of the One in whom we trust is reliable: "Faith shows the reality of what we hope for; it is the evidence of things we cannot see" (Hebrews 11:1). The author of Hebrews shows us the forward projection of faith—that not only do those who practice faith trust in God's goodness, but they understand that what they work toward may not be realized in their lifetimes.

This was certainly true of Zelophehad's daughters; they secured land that the next generations would enjoy. In this way, they had an eternal perspective on their work. God often calls the marginalized and overlooked to pioneer a new way forward for others. They may not even see the fruit of their labor, but they persist with a godly perseverance for the sake of others.

> All these people died still believing what God had promised them. They did not receive what was promised, but they saw it all from a distance and welcomed it. They agreed that they were foreigners and nomads here on earth. (Hebrews 11:13)

When I consider this truth, I think of one particular prayer request I've labored over for many decades. I had to rest in knowing that God would work it out in his timing, even if I didn't see the fruit of my prayers. I cannot tell you how many agonized prayers I have prayed, how many tears I shed over this issue, but I did it because of God's love for people. The Apostle Peter tells us that

> the Lord isn't really slow about his promise, as some people think. No, he is being patient for your sake. He does not want anyone to be destroyed, but wants everyone to repent. (2 Peter 3:9)

When God finally answered those longsuffering prayers after decades of pleading, I was shocked. (I shouldn't have been. I should've had faith like Zelophehad's daughters, who saw far into the future and hoped that their progeny would have security and land.)

We can find our community.

The sisters did not isolate from one another and lament their plight privately. Instead, they banded together to make a united front. Whereas the community seemed to go on as if nothing was awry, or flat-out didn't notice their problem, these women knew they had to work together to find a solution.

When we feel unnoticed or that our situation is unacknowledged, our tendency is to isolate. For me, when I've been harmed by others or dismissed, I tend to cocoon into myself and rehash all the issues over and over in my mind. This rumination does little to help me see the situation proactively (or even accurately). A few years ago, I was not only overlooked in a relationship, but maligned and attacked through email. Initially, I let the shock of it all overcome me, but soon realized I could not bear this alone, nor could I discern where I was in error because the one who accused me was quite adamant. The Scripture is clear on this. Paul writes,

> Dear brothers and sisters, if another believer is overcome by some sin, you who are godly should gently and humbly help that person back onto the right path. And be careful not to fall into the same temptation yourself.

> Share each other's burdens, and in this way obey the law of Christ. (Galatians 6:1–2)

We need others to help us find our fault in volatile situations because we are simply too close to it to find it in our pain. But we also need others to bear our burdens, to help us sift through our pain and find Jesus in the midst of it.

When we are unseen or dismissed, the resulting relational wound requires a relational cure. Even though it is scary to reapproach relationships after you've been harmed in one, it is the pathway back to healing. As I've mentioned in other books, what has wounded you (a negative relationship) is what heals you (a good, strong relationship). Isolation only breeds setbacks. Good community helps you move forward toward a healthier place.

Truths about Noticed You

- You can weather the pain of being unnoticed when you have a circle of friends.
- God is a God of justice; you can rely on that.
- God welcomes you to tell him and others your needs.
- Persistence, petition, and perseverance are all traits God uses to help you move through the pain of being unnoticed toward mental, spiritual, emotional, and relational health.
- God sees your plight.

Questions for Discussion

1. What about this story of the five daughters of Zelophehad encouraged you?

2. What surprised you?
3. Look back on your life. When have you had to stand up for yourself concerning an injustice? What happened?
4. What role does community and friendships play in your life today? How has that changed in the past ten years?
5. What does the story of these daughters teach you about God's compassion and care?

CHAPTER FOUR

Deborah, the Dismayed One

Under the rule of Jabin of Hazor, the nation of Israel suffered. The Canaanites' twisted commander, Sisera, seemed to delight in concocting new cruelties. He often boasted of his nine hundred iron chariots and took great delight in pressing the Israelites into humiliating submission. Deborah knew this in her gut. She had heard the cries of her people, beseeching God for deliverance from Sisera's twisted ways.

All she could do was remain faithful to the calling God had bestowed upon her—to judge this rapscallion nation now bent under Sisera's oppression as she sat under what folks called the Palm of Deborah, nestled in the hill country between Ramah and Bethel. From morning to evening, she would carefully weigh the words and complaints of her people, asking God to give her wisdom to judge well. The task ahead of her each day loomed large, and she felt the burden of it all, much like a shepherd bearing the burden of care for his flock's every need.

Today, though, she sensed the importance of summoning Barak from central Kedesh to her palm stand in the land of Naphtali. The previous evening, the Lord had given her an urgent message for him. *Deliverance was at hand!*

When Barak arrived, she took note of his appearance—a strong, capable warrior. She smiled. Yes, this would be the one the Lord had summoned to bring deliverance!

"This is what the Lord, the God of Israel, commands you," she told him. "Call out ten thousand warriors from the tribes of Naphtali and Zebulun at Mount Tabor. And I will call out Sisera, commander of Jabin's army, along with his chariots and warriors, to the Kishon River. There I will give you victory over him."

Barak looked away, fidgeting with his hands. For a long time, he silently gazed up at the sky as if to beg God to choose someone else. Finally, he said, "I will go, but only if you go with me."

Deborah shook her head, wiping the sweat from her brow. Throughout her life she had known God to be faithful and strong on behalf of those who felt weak and incapable. His character was consistent and intentional. She prayed briefly, not wanting to answer Barak hastily. If she were to go, she wanted the Lord of Hosts on her side. But why would Barak not exercise such faith on his own? Why would he ask such a thing of her? Dismay ate at her.

Still, she sought the Lord, letting her silence keep Barak waiting. When she felt the sense of *shalom* God often sent her way when she faced decisions like this, she said, "Very well. I will go with you. But you will receive no honor in this venture, for the Lord's victory over Sisera will be at the hands of a woman."

Together they ventured toward Kedesh, where Barak, true to his word, gathered an army of ten thousand warriors from the tribes God had instructed, then headed east toward the slopes of Mount

Tabor. They settled into a strong position on the mountain so they could see when Sisera and his army approached from the west.

And approach they did, leaving Harosheth-haggoyim to camp at the Kishon River. At first, the warriors of Israel only spied dust moving toward the river valley below, but when the pounding of hooves and the rankling of chariots finally reached their ears, they brought fear with them.

Deborah knew she needed to infuse Barak with the strength of the Lord if they were to prevail against such a volatile enemy. "Get ready!" she shouted. "This is the day the Lord will give you victory over Sisera, for the Lord is marching ahead of you!"

Barak nodded, then led his troops from the security of Mount Tabor's slopes down into battle. The moment they charged, God did exactly as He had promised: Sisera's army suddenly fell into panic, even going so far as to attack each other. Deborah saw Sisera leap from his chariot and run into the wilderness alone. *Coward*, she thought.

Barak pressed further east, leading his army toward the stronghold of Harosheth-haggoyim, slaying all the Canaanite warriors in their path. Not even one of Sisera's infantry was left alive. Their God had given them a stunning victory.

Deborah accompanied Barak on the search for Sisera in enemy territory. Though the area was populated by fellow Israelites, the tribes there shared a friendly alliance with King Jabin, Israel's oppressor. Surely these turncoat families would protect Sisera and hide him well. And though the day's battle had been won, they were not entirely out of danger.

Several fruitless hours passed. But then, a woman who called herself Jael approached Barak. Blood covered her hands, and an inexplicable look of satisfaction covered her half-veiled face.

"Come," she said, motioning toward a nearby tent, "and I will show you the man you are looking for."

They followed her through the camp toward her tent. Deborah half expected to be ambushed, but when they reached Jael's tent, there lay Sisera—quite dead, a long tent peg pounded through his temple into the earth. His eyes stared straight ahead, and his mouth gaped. Blood still wept from the wound, reddening the earth beneath. The man who had tortured and taunted the Israelites for far too long would offer no such rebellion in death.

Jael's decisive act encouraged the Israelite army. Eventually, they destroyed King Jabin and his empire.

When they returned from their exploits, Deborah and Barak sang a song to the God who had delivered their people: "Israel's leaders took charge, and the people gladly followed. Praise the Lord!"

And it was true. God's word to Deborah had proven to be both precise and authentic.

"Listen, you kings!" Deborah sang, "Pay attention, you mighty rulers! For I will sing to the Lord. I will make music to the Lord, the God of Israel." Her song was neither about her nor about Barak, but about God's victory and ability to deliver his people from those far too strong for them.

"Lord," she trilled, "when you set out from Seir and marched across the fields of Edom, the earth trembled, and the cloudy skies poured down rain. The mountains quaked in the presence of the Lord, the God of Mount Sinai—in the presence of the Lord, the God of Israel."

Deborah motioned for her countrymen to join her with stringed instruments, and women and children began to dance in celebration. "In the days of Shamgar son of Anath, and in the days of Jael, people avoided the main roads, and travelers stayed on winding pathways."

It was true. They'd become a furtive, frightened people, avoiding central pathways for fear of attack by bandits who would go unpunished by Jabin's corrupt regime.

Barak sang the song's next verse. "There were few people left in the villages of Israel—until Deborah arose as a mother for Israel. When Israel chose new gods, war erupted at the city gates. Yet not a shield or spear could be seen among forty thousand warriors in Israel!"

All great songs were stories, Deborah knew, and this one was fraught with conflict and pain. The Israelites had trudged their way through life back then, giving into fear so often that they had forgotten how to fight. They had resigned themselves to superstitious beliefs in gods that could not even deliver a scroll, much less a victory against a stronger army.

But Deborah was thrilled by what had happened that day. "My heart," she sang, "is with the commanders of Israel, with those who volunteered for war. Praise the Lord!" Those brave ten thousand had exercised faith in God's abilities to deliver them. This she felt in her gut.

This next line she sang to the children as a cautionary tale. "Consider this, you who ride on fine donkeys, you who sit on fancy saddle blankets, and you who walk along the road. Listen to the village musicians gathered at the watering holes. They recount the righteous victories of the Lord and the victories of his villagers in Israel. Then," she looked at the children and smiled, "the people of the Lord marched down to the city gates." With this, the children marched in circles, as if they were encircling Jericho again all these years later.

The children chanted, "Wake up, Deborah, wake up! Wake up, wake up, and sing a song!" as Deborah clapped her hands.

They continued, "Arise, Barak! Lead your captives away, son of Abinoam!" Barak tapped his feet to their rhythm.

The nation danced and sang, demonstrating their gratitude to God.

Deborah continued singing. "Down from Tabor marched the few against the nobles. The people of the Lord marched down against mighty warriors. They came down from Ephraim—a land that once belonged to the Amalekites; they followed you, Benjamin, with your troops. From Makir the commanders marched down; from Zebulun came those who carry a commander's staff." Recounting God's faithfulness gladdened them all so much that it almost felt as if the Festival of Booths were upon them.

They continued the song, recounting the bravery of their warriors and Barak and Deborah—but they also sang about the tribe of Reuben's indecision in the matter. Melodies arose about the fickleness of the other tribes who failed to assist them in the fight—how Gilead had remained on the other side of the Jordan River and Dan chose to stay home. Asher remained encamped at the seashore, unmoved by their cousins' plight.

Deborah continued, her voice rising in a crescendo. "But Zebulun risked his life, as did Naphtali, on the heights of the battlefield." She made eye contact with the exhausted warriors, conveying her gratitude. Of God's supreme part of the victory, she sang, "The stars fought from heaven. The stars in their orbits fought against Sisera. The Kishon River swept them away—that ancient torrent, the Kishon."

And then she included the words that she had spoken to her soul as they approached the enemy, the melody that had kept her in step with the Almighty's abilities, though she felt her own to be small and insignificant: "March on with courage, my soul!"

A cry arose from the camp, as if those words reignited their own courage. With their God, all things were possible.

She musically cursed Meroz and others who did not help God's people—but then the melody turned from the minor key to major as she sang of the bravery of Jael. "Most blessed among women is Jael, the wife of Heber the Kenite. May she be blessed above all women who live in tents." Another cry arose from the camp as she sang of how Jael lulled mighty Sisera to slumber with a bowl of milk and yogurt, then felled him with a rudimentary tool—a tent peg—fueled by holy strength and the weight of a hammer.

Deborah then sang from Sisera's mother's point of view: "From the window Sisera's mother looked out." Deborah put her hand as a shade above her forehead. The children nearby mimicked her. "Through the window she watched for his return, saying, 'Why is his chariot so long in coming? Why don't we hear the sound of chariot wheels?'"

"Indeed, why?" shouted Barak.

"Her wise women answer, and she repeats these words to herself: 'They must be dividing the captured plunder—with a woman or two for every man. There will be colorful robes for Sisera, and colorful, embroidered robes for me. Yes, the plunder will include colorful robes embroidered on both sides.'" With this, Deborah swirled the skirt of her long tunic in circles. "There will be no colorful robes for our enemies today!"

"Indeed!" Barak said.

Deborah ended the song as a blessing over a people no longer oppressed. "Lord, may all your enemies die like Sisera! But may those who love you rise like the sun in all its power!"

After the celebrations, Deborah resumed her position under her palm tree. With less fear, more freedom, and the knowledge that God would fight on their behalf, the nation experienced God's favor and peace from war for the next forty glorious years.

The Biblical Narrative

It's important to know the context of Deborah's fascinating story to glean all we can from her example, found primarily in Judges 4 and

5. She existed in the period of the judges, a time after Israel settled in Canaan but before the people insisted on having a king. This story takes place 1,300 years before Christ's birth. We see this haunting refrain throughout the book of Judges: "In those days Israel had no king; all the people did whatever seemed right in their own eyes" (Judges 17:6, restated slightly differently in Judges 21:25—the very last verse of the book). You can hear the ominous tones there. To quell the chaos of unrestricted immorality, the nation had judges to watch over communal affairs and offer counsel in matters of the Law.

Scholars often refer to this time in Israel's history as the "cycle of the judges"—because there was, indeed, a cycle: Israel would rebel against God by chasing idols. God would then send a prophet or a judge to call the people out on that, and judgment would come crashing down. Israel would cry out during the pain of that judgment and vow to do better. They would repent. And then all would be well—until another idol caught their attention, and then the cycle would begin again. Albert Baylis, professor at Multnomah University, contrasts the difference between the time when Joshua was leading the nation to victories over pagan Canaanite tribes and the time of the judges:

> If the book of Joshua is a flowing stream, fresh and invigorating with direction and power, then Judges is the river that turns sluggish and muddy, its polluted water ultimately spiraling down a storm drain.[1]

But Deborah interrupted this cycle. Her story is told in Judges 4 and 5—the latter being comprised mostly of the song she sang to celebrate God's deliverance. Judges 4:1–2 says,

> After Ehud's death, the Israelites again did evil in the Lord's sight. So the Lord turned them over to King Jabin of Hazor, a Canaanite king. The commander of his army was Sisera, who lived in Harosheth-haggoyim.

The phrase "did evil" is in the active voice, which means it was a deliberate choice to follow idols, with the people willingly forsaking their God in favor of lesser gods. Into this quagmire Deborah arose as the nation's fourth judge. In that role, she operated much as Moses had centuries earlier: Judges 4:5 says, "She would sit under the Palm of Deborah, between Ramah and Bethel in the hill country of Ephraim, and the Israelites would go to her for judgment." Similarly, Exodus 18:13 reads, "The next day, Moses took his seat to hear the people's disputes against each other. They waited before him from morning till evening." Both were seated, both heard pleas and causes, both labored all day, and both rendered judgments.

Deborah means "honeybee" or "wasp," which reflects a bit of her feisty character—one who can be sweet and yet still deliver a zinger when necessary. She calls herself "a mother in Israel" (see Judges 5:7), and then, ironically, mocks Sisera's mother in her song. She is described as a prophetess, a judge, and a military leader for the nation.

Even though she plays all these powerful roles, she is still mentioned in the biblical text as the wife of Lappodith; she still operated within the nation's patriarchal structure, a pathway of being overlooked that was infused in her culture. Interestingly, Deborah is the only woman who the Bible tells us was both a prophet and judge; the only other person to occupy both offices simultaneously was Samuel, who anointed the first and second kings of Israel at the end of the time of the judges.

Like Miriam, whom we studied earlier, Deborah was musically gifted. Her song is sheer Hebrew poetry, and it is both lengthy and pithy.

Unlike the other women we'll study in this book, Deborah did experience doses of honor in her context. She played an important role in Israel's history. She led with cunning and grace. So how does she fit into this idea of being unseen?

As I studied her life, I came across many male theologians who asserted that it was only because the men of Deborah's time didn't step up to lead that Deborah became a judge. God had to resort to Plan B—a woman—they claim. Instead of doing a careful reading of the entire Bible, throughout which God often affirms women, these theologians relegated Deborah to second-class status, unrecognized for her talents and only placed where she was because God couldn't find a man to do the job.

As women, we often *are* overlooked by church leaders simply because of our gender. I recently lamented to a male pastor, "I can't seem to use my gifts in my own church context. It's exhausting. I must travel overseas to use the gifts God has given me."

"Can you mentor women by going to lunch with them once in a while?" he asked me. His implication was that he felt there was a hole not being filled there, and I could take this responsibility off his to-do list (to find someone). I felt like he had just thrown me an overchewed bone.

Then he told me that when he retired, he thought he would "do some consulting." What he was trying to say was that I could just retire from my job, then do whatever I wanted as a ministry.

The problem was that, as a woman, I have not been given formal "ministry opportunities" in my church. It was a statement of privilege for him to say he could just consult. I could not make such a choice because I don't have the ministry experience required to become a consultant for other women about ministry-related matters—at least, not any outside of children's ministries or women's ministries, which often seem to be the only areas where women are traditionally welcomed to serve.

This is why Deborah's story gives me hope.

God *chose* her. She was not his second choice because no man would step up. After all, God chose Barak, too, as well as the ten-thousand-man army. Deborah was the right person for the incredibly difficult job of leading the nation daily, judging their disputes, and calling them to military victory—three roles typically filled by males. God chose Deborah as part of his multifaceted plan, which hinted at his longing all along—that Israel would become a city on a hill, a beacon to the vulnerable, a signpost pointing the way to the God who loves all humanity.

How This Applies to Dismayed You

So what can we learn from Deborah when we are dismayed at the faithlessness around us, and we feel we haven't had the chance to practice our faith in public?

We can know God.

To operate as a prophetess, Deborah had to know God. She had to pursue him, listen for his voice, and know his character. She had to study who he was and what kind of law he promoted. She had to have a robust understanding of his justice. This would be particularly helpful when injustice arose in the idolatry-prone nation. If we know God well, we can know his heart, then act or speak accordingly. Hosea, the minor prophet, encouraged this kind of pursuit, which likely typified Deborah:

> Oh, that we might know the Lord! Let us press on to know him. He will respond to us as surely as the arrival

> of dawn or the coming of rains in early spring. (Hosea 6:3)

When we are underestimated, we can rest assured that God knows even the most intricate details of our lives. We press in to know him, but the good news is that he already knows us. David reminds us,

> O Lord, you have examined my heart and know everything about me. You know when I sit down or stand up. You know my thoughts even when I'm far away. (Psalm 139:1–2)

Psalm 139 serves as a bedrock reminder of the intimate way God knows us. What's even more encouraging is that, although we think we know ourselves well, he knows us even better. This means we can rest in the knowledge that his sovereign plan will fit us perfectly. Nothing escapes his notice—particularly the injustice we may suffer at times.

We can settle into God's calling.

God specifically called Deborah, which most likely informed her wholehearted obedience. The task ahead of her was participating in leading the nation into war against a formidable enemy, and yet, because she was assured of God's call, she didn't hesitate to obey. But we may miss something as we watch her story unfold: Before her heroic charge, Deborah spent an unspecified period of time sitting under her palm tree, day in and day out. She had spent hours listening to people's personal disputes and troubles, seeking God for wisdom for each complaint. She developed her muscle for responding to him in those times. She wasn't called in one moment, and then co-led ten-thousand men into battle in the next. In our culture of instant gratification, it's hard for us to walk through the discipline of apprenticeship the way many heroes of the faith—including Joseph, Moses, King David, the major and minor prophets, and even Jesus himself—did. All had long periods of time between the calling and its fulfillment.

When I counsel authors as a literary agent, I remind them of the importance of going back to the moment when they *knew*-knew-knew that God had called them to write. Because after that, hundreds of macro and micro rejections will test a writer's literary mettle. I remind them to settle themselves in their calling because this will help them endure the trials ahead of them. But we don't have to be writers to appreciate this practice. In a fiery trial, we must train our minds to go back to that place of calling, reminding ourselves of why we do what we do and who we do it for. God himself uniquely created us to do this, and no one else can do it in the same manner that we can. We are necessary.

We didn't call ourselves to kingdom work—*God* did. Jesus said, "You didn't choose me. I chose you. I appointed you to go and produce lasting fruit, so that the Father will give you whatever you ask for, using my name" (John 15:16). What a surprising and beautiful promise! When we feel entirely underestimated, we can remind ourselves that God chose us. He has appointed us to carry out the tasks ahead of us. We see the intricacy of our own creation, the artistic precision God used to fashion us, in Ephesians 2:10:

> For we are God's masterpiece. He has created us anew in Christ Jesus, so we can do the good things he planned for us long ago.

As he fashioned Deborah, he uniquely qualified her for prophecy, judging, and warfare. She simply walked into that place of calling to the *nth* degree.

Nowhere do you see Deborah lamenting the fact that she was a woman. Nor do you see others around her arguing, "Well, there aren't enough men around, so God was forced to choose a woman." God equipped her. She exercised her gifts, and then the Lord brought divine deliverance to her people through them. A blogger makes this interesting point:

> I wonder how the Israelites felt about Deborah. Did anyone walk out on her? Did anyone condemn her for speaking on behalf of God? Did anyone encourage her to take more interest in her domestic duties? We don't know. What we do know is that it was the Lord's will to use her as a leader of God's people to deliver them (with Barak's help as general). Judges does not offer a command to promote women, but it only takes one example like Deborah to show that women are just as capable in leadership as men. Leadership did not suppress Deborah's femininity but gave her an important setting to be "motherly protector" (5:7).[2]

When we know God's character,
we can move forward with confidence.

Deborah, as mentioned above, knew the character of God, which fueled her gutsy confidence. She did not hesitate to move against a brutal enemy that was considered unbeatable. She understood that God's strength far surpassed the enemy's supposed might. Similarly, the more we press in to know the Lord (to use Hosea's language), the longer we see him act faithfully, and the more that knowledge builds our trust muscle. We may not have confidence in our own abilities, but we can have confidence in God's power. When we are underestimated, though, that confidence can wane. We must be careful not to allow the voices of others to shout more loudly than heaven does. The author of Hebrews cautions us,

> So do not throw away this confident trust in the Lord. Remember the great reward it brings you! Patient endurance is what you need now, so that you will continue to do God's will. Then you will receive all that he has promised. (Hebrews 10:35–36)

We are drained of confidence by the discouraging words of others, and if we ruminate on those long enough, they become highways carved into our thinking, our default way of seeing the world. I can't tell you how many times throughout childhood and young adulthood I felt left out and overlooked. The taunts of others shouted more loudly than any sort of esteem I had. It was not until I met Jesus at fifteen that I began to slowly reform my view of myself. As a person who's experienced multiple traumatic events, I seemed to have no bright future—only a path of walking into more pain. But Jesus spoke life over me. He chose me. He forgave me. He pursued me. He noticed me. He loved me (and he still does!) When I said that first prayer to him under a starry Northwestern sky, something cataclysmically shifted in me, and I had a revolution of the heart. No longer forsaken and forgotten, I was now sought out and set free. This eventually fueled my confidence when the storms of life pelted me with hail or when others said negative things to or about me.

Deborah may have been bewildered at the lack of faith around her, but God esteemed her and affirmed her faith in him. He chose her, called her, empowered her to conquer, and then to sing a victory song. Friend, you may feel underestimated, forgotten, forsaken. But God esteems you. He chooses you. He calls you. He will empower you to conquer the obstacles in your daily life, then worship him in the glowing aftermath.

Truths about Esteemed You

- You cannot reverse the calling God has on your life.
- Others may underestimate you, but God's strength is always available to help you face your trials.
- Singing worship songs is an appropriate response to a victory in your life.
- Apprenticeship follows calling, but often a long period of time passes between the initial calling and its fulfillment.
- Being a woman is not a negative in God's Kingdom. He chooses women to do amazing tasks.

Questions for Discussion

1. What do you think Deborah learned in the mundane aspects of judging others' problems?
2. Why do you think waiting while in apprenticeship is not considered a favorable way to do things today?
3. When has God called you to do a seemingly impossible task? How did he counterintuitively bring victory?
4. As you look back over the past decade of your life, when have you "pressed on to know the Lord" most fiercely? What prompted that pursuit?
5. What does Deborah's obedience teach you about who God calls?

CHAPTER FIVE

Abigail, the Trapped One

Abigail felt the weight of grief that permeated the land so heavily that it seemed to seep into the crevices and rocks of Israel. Samuel, the prophet, was dead, and there was no resurrecting him. He had been buried, she knew, in his homeland in Ramah. Abigail heard that as they laid him to rest, the sun had darkened and the clouds had wept.

It made perfect sense to her that David, whom Samuel had anointed as king, would mourn in the wilderness, but she did not expect him and his entourage to show up on her doorstep. Maon, a small town on the outskirts of Carmel, did not boast much beyond that. But what it did have was Nabal.

Known as the man with three thousand sheep and a thousand goats, Nabal ruled his tiny empire with both force and greed. Years ago, when Abigail's father had told her she was to be married off to him, she had withdrawn to the hills and wept. She knew Nabal to be a hard man—exacting, calculated, and evil. *Why would Father think this a good match?* But she had neither the means nor the will to displease her father, so she wept her tears before the Lord on the mountainside, pulling at her hair. But when she returned home to accept the inevitability of her fate, she wrapped her hair neatly into her head covering, dried her tears, and faced her future with solemn resignation.

At night, she would study Nabal's face as he slept, noting the contours of his profile. Even in sleep, the hardness won. His mouth formed a firm, unmoving line, and his brows scowled even in repose. He was a descendent of a faithful man, their ancestor Caleb—one of the ten spies Moses sent into the Promised Land. Only he and Joshua had faith enough to believe the nation of Israel could swiftly conquer Canaan; the other eight had melted in fear. Nabal had inherited Caleb's confident nature, but not his faith in God's ability. He was fully confident of only one thing: his ability to make wealth. It had been his one compelling obsession since childhood, she knew.

Sheep-shearing season had always been stressful for Abigail because it meant Nabal would be counting everything—sheep pelts and potential pounds of mutton. Money, money, money. And with money came celebration—later in the evening, strong drink.

"You!" Nabal barked at a young shepherd. "You're moving too slowly! Get over here now or I'll send you away—and without pay."

Abigail noted the boy's wide eyes were holding tears that had nearly released. Later that afternoon, in a quiet moment away from her calculating husband's gaze, she would slip a day's wage into his pouch and thank him, apologizing for Nabal's rudeness. This was her lot, she knew—to clean up her husband's physical and relational messes. She worked hard at managing his life and business, trying to do everything perfectly so he wouldn't turn his wrath on her. But even when she performed exactly as God had empowered her to do, it was never enough for Nabal. He always found fault with someone—except himself.

Abigail lived in a state approaching panic, her heartbeat resonating in her chest, rising and falling on her husband's mercurial moods.

One sheep-shearing day, Abigail noticed a caravan of men coming their way. She feared what Nabal would say or do to them, so she tried to reach them first.

Smack! Nabal's hand left a welt across her face. "Go home," he told her. "I will attend to this."

She touched her cheek, then retreated, hoping to hear the conversation. She had to be vigilant to clean up after Nabal's nastiness. But this time, she could not. She had been banished to their home to nurse her wound.

But later, one of Nabal's servants told her all the details.

"There were ten men who approached our master," he said. "The man in charge had a pleasant face and a calm demeanor. But only a scowl crossed Nabal's face. As you've seen before, our master believes every person to be a threat. He expected others to be as himself—a thief and a cheat."

Abigail nodded. "Tell me the rest."

"Peace and prosperity to you, your family, and everything you own!" said the pleasant man who had come from afar.

Nabal gave him a hard stare. The man swallowed, then continued. "I am told that it is sheep-shearing time."

Nabal's only response was to roll his eyes and point at the bleating sheep around them.

The man shifted, took a deep breath, and said, "While your shepherds stayed among us near Carmel, we never harmed them, and nothing was ever stolen from them."

Nabal grunted.

Then the man motioned toward the servants. "Ask your own men, and they will tell you this is true."

Nabal never asked anyone for anything; he *ordered*. But in this case, he did neither. He kept quiet.

"So would you be kind to us since we have come at a time of celebration? Please share any provisions you might have on hand with us and with your friend David," the man said.

Nabal paced closer to David's men until he stood nose-to-nose with the messenger, holding his gaze with a hard, cold look. "Who is this fellow *David*?" he spat. He ran a circle around the group of ten, which seemed to give his anger momentum. "Who does this son of Jesse think he is?"

The man's eyes widened as he looked around him at his companions. His hand balled into a fist. His temple throbbed, but he said nothing.

Then Nabal stepped closer. "There are lots of servants these days who run away from their masters. Should I take my bread and my water and my meat that I've slaughtered for my shearers and give it to a band of outlaws who come from who knows where?"

He pointed in the direction they had come from, then made a swatting motion for them to leave his presence at once.

"Thank you for telling me the story," Abigail told the servant.

The man shook his head. "He screamed insults at them!"

"It is what he does," she said. "It is in his nature."

"But" the servant said, shaking his head, "these men have been very good to us, and we never suffered any harm from them. Nothing was stolen from us the whole time they were with us. In fact, day and night, they were like a wall of protection for us and the sheep."

Abigail nodded. A tear slipped down her cheek.

The servant held her gaze, fear glistening in his eyes. "You need to figure out what to do, for there is going to be trouble for our master and his whole family. He's so ill-tempered that no one can even talk to him!"

Oh, dear God. All Nabal's life had been about him alone. But now his selfish rebellion would ruin not only him, but her and all their faithful servants as well. She had to do something—anything—to quell David's justified fury. But what?

She thought of Nabal's wealth and the importance of showing hospitality to David's weary men. She looked around the compound, scanning for Nabal. If he saw what she did behind his back, he would kill her. In a rush, Abigail gathered two hundred loaves of fresh bread, two large wineskins full of aged wine, and put them into saddle bags. She then carefully wrapped the mutton from five slaughtered sheep and put it into more saddle bags. There was enough there for at least three donkeys to carry.

"Quick," she told one of her servant girls. "Gather as much of a bushel of roasted grain as you can find. Put it in this sack."

She rounded out the stow of provisions with a hundred clusters of raisins and two hundred fig cakes. The donkeys hee-hawed in protest, but she instructed capable servants on what to do. "Go on ahead with these donkeys," she told them. "I will follow you shortly."

She knew she would overtake them, as her donkey only carried the load of one small woman, so she gathered herself, smoothed her head covering, and rode quickly toward David's encampment. She had to navigate a risky ravine, but the donkey was surefooted, even as the sun dipped lower in the sky. The acoustics in the ravine carried the voices of David's men her way.

After rounding a bend, she saw the entourage ahead. David was addressing them animatedly.

"A lot of good it did to help this fellow!" he shouted. "We protected his flocks in the wilderness, and nothing he owned was lost or stolen. But he has repaid me evil for good." He lifted a spear skyward. "May God strike and kill me if even one man of his household is still alive tomorrow morning!"

Abigail kicked the donkey beneath her into a faster trot. Reaching David, she dismounted and bowed before him, silently asking God for words that would sway his heart.

"I accept all blame in this matter, my lord," she said. "Please listen to what I have to say."

David motioned for her to rise.

She stood, wiping the tears from her face, and taking a settling breath. "I know Nabal is a wicked and ill-tempered man; please don't pay any attention to him," she said. "He is a fool, just as his name suggests. But I never even saw the young men you sent."

The braying of donkeys interrupted her speech. She turned, noting animals laden with provisions had just arrived.

"Now, my lord, as sure as the Lord lives and you yourself live, since the Lord has kept you from murdering and taking vengeance into your own hands, let all your enemies and those who try to harm you be as cursed as Nabal is." She pointed to the donkeys. "And here is a present that I, your servant, have brought to you and your young men. Please forgive me if I have offended you in any way. The Lord will surely reward you with a lasting dynasty, for you are fighting his battles. And you have not done wrong throughout your entire life."

David stepped back, shooting a look at his men. But he said nothing.

Abigail hoped her words had salvaged the situation, but she could not be sure. She steadied herself. "Even when you are chased by those who seek to kill you, your life is safe in the care of the Lord your God, secure in his treasure pouch!" She felt the power of God rise within her and sensed the encouragement he wanted to share with David, his servant. "But the lives of your enemies will disappear like stones shot from a sling! When the Lord has done all he promised and has made you leader of Israel, don't let this be a blemish on your record. Then your conscience won't have to bear the staggering burden of needless bloodshed and vengeance. And when the Lord has done these great things for you, please remember me, your servant!" She stopped talking, but her heart continued to pound a worried rhythm in her chest.

David smiled.

Oh, thank God.

"Praise the Lord, the God of Israel, who has sent you to meet me today!" he said. "Thank God for your good sense! Bless you for keeping me from murder and from carrying out vengeance with my own hands." He looked at his hands as if he were questioning them.

The strain in Abigail's neck and shoulders eased. David had perceived her heart and knew that she had heeded the nudging of God to bring him gifts.

He gathered his men around him, as if to address them and her at the same time. "For I swear by the Lord, the God of Israel, who has kept me from hurting you, that if you had not hurried out to meet me, not one of Nabal's men would still be alive tomorrow morning."

The precariousness of their situation was not lost on Abigail. She was grateful for the Lord's empowerment and the donkeys' swift trotting to get there in time. She backed away from David, then stroked the spikey mane of her humble steed.

David walked over to the group of donkeys carrying food and wine. He nodded, accepting Abigail's gifts. "Return home in peace. I have heard what you said. We will not kill your husband."

As she turned to leave, she heard the joyful exclamations of David's men over the provisions. She smiled, thanking God for his protection.

A different sound of celebration greeted her as she neared home, and her stomach knotted. When Nabal drank, she often bore the brunt of his angry fits. And if he found out what she had done, he might even kill her in a fit of drunken rage.

She spent the night not sleeping, but keeping watch, hoping Nabal would not even speak to her. He passed out in the early morning hours, and she thankfully let him sleep as long as he would, regardless of how high the sun rose in the sky outside their tent. But when he finally began to stir, God told her she must reveal what she'd done. She hoped knowing she had placated the mighty David would soothe Nabal, but deep inside, she worried. Anyone who did anything outside the strict confines of his detailed instructions paid for it—often with their lives. There had never been any room for grace in the household of Nabal, she knew.

She kept her voice low, singing as she prepared his morning meal. She swallowed, then sat beside him. "Nabal," she said.

"What is it?" There was neither anger nor affection in his tone. His head seemed to be hurting from the previous night's activities.

Abigail recounted the entire story quickly so she could get to the part where David had said he would spare Nabal's life.

When she finished speaking, the left side of Nabal's face suddenly froze, and drool slipped from the corner of his mouth.

"Are you not well?" she asked.

But Nabal did not answer, and his eyes registered nothing. He breathed, but his mind had died as he lay paralyzed. Abigail called servants to help him back to his bed.

Nabal never stirred again. In ten days—one for every one of David's men he had denied provisions—he was dead.

How would Abigail live now? What could she do? How would she provide for the servants? While they could find other work, she could not. Her job had been to take care of Nabal—and as grateful as she was to no longer deal with his wrath, that job had suddenly ceased to exist. She tried not to worry, but she could not help herself.

A single vulture wheeled overhead, circling above her like a noose.

Several days later, a caravan approached her home from the direction of Carmel. She noticed the men in it wore the regalia of David, as before. One man approached her. "David has sent us to take you back to marry him," he said.

So this is Your answer, Lord. She hadn't even allowed herself to think of such an audacious answer to prayer, but now here it was, standing before her. She would no longer be a widow, but the wife of the next king of Israel!

She bowed low before the man who had brought the news. "I, your servant, would be happy to marry David," she said. "I would even be willing to become a slave, washing the feet of his servants!"

As quickly as she had gathered supplies to deter David's vengeance, she summoned five servant girls to be her attendants, mounted her faithful donkey, and followed David's messengers to Carmel.

Abigail became a bride for a second time in her life—but this time to the future king, rather than a fool.

Abigail's life with David and his men in Ziklag was a slice of domesticity; she focused on raising their son, young Chileab, while David's other wife, Ahinoam, did the same with her son Amnon. Though they all knew that King Saul's mind had become unhinged—he'd been trying to kill David for years and had even sought the ungodly counsel of a witch in trying to retain the throne of Israel—those things barely touched them in their desert in Philistine territory.

Their most pressing concern now was that David, once again, had volunteered for war at the behest of the Philistines, so they waited for his return. Abigail's stomach lurched as she considered the possibilities.

When she heard the rumble of camels' hoofbeats outside, she looked out, expecting to see David coming home with the spoils of war. To her horror, instead, she saw a hoard of Amalekite warriors staring at her.

They ripped her, Chileab, Ahinoam, and Amnon from their homes with a violence that took her breath away—and then set fire to the whole camp. Their hands were bound, and ropes connected them as they stumbled together after the Amalekites' camels. She cried out, but no one seemed to hear her.

After a long trek of fear and thirst, Abigail stopped crying then, but she did not know why. *I must be strong for Chileab,* she told herself.

Eventually, as they were pulled along in the caravan of hopelessness, Abigail steadied herself. *I must remain strong for Chileab,* she told herself again. She forced herself to press on, her feet blistering and the sun beating on her uncovered face. She could not sing. She could not talk. She could only pray for rescue.

Three days passed on the hot, dusty trail. On the third day, Abigail had a moment to comfort her son, to sing songs over him to calm his tears, but it was nearly impossible to be heard over the raucous celebration taking place outside their prison tent. The Amalekites had taken to drinking, carousing, and dancing with hysterical joy. They threw their plunder—all the precious implements, jars, and valuable assets they had stolen from the homes of David and his men—as if they were trash. People didn't take care of that which they stole, Abigail knew.

A rumbling noise erupted over the revelry—and then, the merrymakers' shouts turned to cries.

David.

"Hurry," Abigail told her son. "Father is here to rescue us." The boy's eyes lit up at the word. She wrapped him in her arms and peeked outside the tent.

There stood her husband—the one meant to be king. He and his mighty men began slaughtering the Amalekites like prey, even as some of them tried to escape on camelback.

When all finally fell quiet, David found her.

"Are you well?" he asked. "And my son?"

She nodded, then presented young Chileab to his father. The family embraced as the moon rose into the star-dotted sky.

As they followed victorious path back toward home, they came across a group of two hundred of David's men, whom Abigail later found out had not been in the fight at the Amalekite camp. Instead, they had stayed at a brook, resting from exhaustion. Some of David's other men were embittered by this. One said, "They didn't go with us, so they can't have any of the plunder we recovered. Give them their wives and children, and tell them to be gone."

She wondered briefly how David would handle the situation. She looked at him, and he caught her gaze.

"No, my brothers!" he said. "Don't be selfish with what the Lord has given us. He has kept us safe and helped us defeat the band of raiders that attacked us. Who will listen when you talk like this? We share and share alike—those who go to battle and those who guard the equipment." He made a decree about those who guarded equipment, a law that prevailed in Israel.

Abigail smiled. Perhaps it was her persuasion that made David relent of vengeance with Nabal that instructed him today.

The Biblical Narrative

We learn about Abigail primarily from 1 Samuel 25 and 30, which records a tumultuous time in Israel's history. We burst onto the scene right after the death of Samuel, who had earlier anointed David to be king. No doubt during that time, people would've wondered if Samuel's predictions about David had died with him. What would happen next?

What followed was King Saul's mad antics—chasing David, trying to kill him. In the middle of this campaign of terror, we find David in Carmel, sending his men to a nearby homestead to ask for a favor. Unfortunately, they ask it of a hard, cruel man named Nabal. The rest is detailed in the story referenced above. In a world where women had no personal power, Abigail bursts into the narrative with guts and intelligence.

Although David and his six hundred men had protected Nabal from outside forces when they had first encountered each other (allowing his ranch to flourish), Nabal's response to their simple (and common) request for hospitality was swift and mean-spirited. It was only through Abigail's quick thinking and generosity that he was spared from David's sword.

That being the case, how, exactly, was Abigail overlooked? She seems like a powerful, capable woman. But we cannot forget the circumstances she lived in before the encounter with David's men. Sadly, it is the story of many women today—that of a neglected or abused wife. While the text does not specifically say Nabal was physically abusive toward her, the implication is there. She admits it when she tells David, "I know Nabal is a wicked and ill-tempered man" (1 Samuel 25:25a). The Hebrew word for "wicked" here is *beliyyaal*, "from belî + ya'al: 'not, without' and 'to be of use, worth, or profit.'"[1] He is useless, then. You may recognize that Hebrew word is the same as *Belial*—a synonym for "Satan" used in the New Testament. The word can also mean "scoundrel" or "worthless."

No doubt Abigail was unseen, unnoticed, and unappreciated by her evil husband. The text of 1 Samuel 25:3 reveals much about these two people.

> This man's name was Nabal, and his wife, Abigail, was a sensible and beautiful woman. But Nabal, a descendant of Caleb, was crude and mean in all his dealings.

The word translated "crude" here is *qasheh*. It basically means everything awful: violent, severe, hard, cruel. It's an agricultural term that connotes a difficult yoke or burden borne by oxen—hard labor. The word translated "mean" here is the common Hebrew word *ra*, used to describe the Tree of Knowledge of Good and Evil. It's used to describe the nature of Satan, the serpent seeking to turn humanity away from the Creator. It is the very antithesis of all that is good. In short, Nabal was the worst of humanity—and Abigail had to navigate life alongside this man whose name meant "fool."

It's important, too, to notice some parallels here between Nabal and Saul. Both acted rashly based on their emotions. Both retaliated against people who only extended kindness to them. (Saul continued to chase David even though David had spared his life—twice.) Instead of behaving emotionally, David calmly chooses to rest in God's timing. David learned much about restraint during his time in the wilderness, and Abigail may often have reminded him of those things. She hints at what will happen in David's future when she says prophetically, "The Lord will surely reward you with a lasting dynasty, for you are fighting the Lord's battles" (1 Samuel 25:28b).

How This Applies to Trapped You

So what are we to do when we feel like Abigail? How can we learn from her courage, wisdom, and quick action?

Be someone others turn to for counsel.

To whom did one of Nabal's servants turn when he went off the rails? He ran to Abigail. She must've proven herself to be Nabal's opposite. Where he was hard and evil, she was soft-hearted and kind. Where he was stingy and unfair, she demonstrated generosity and justice. We do not know what made Nabal the way he was. Perhaps he was overlooked too? But he always had a choice about how to behave. Though her relational circumstances were extremely difficult, Abigail chose to emulate the beautiful Hebrew word *hesed*, which means "loyal love and kindness."

No matter what happens to us, no matter how much we're maligned or overlooked, we can always choose to become the kind of people others seek when they are in distress. Of course, the power to do that comes only from the Holy Spirit and our surrendering to God's will. But Abigail reveals to us that our circumstances do not need to make us hard or bitter. When we stay connected to the source of goodness, God himself, we can rise above the pain and become outrageously generous—so much so that others seek us out for help.

Obey God without hesitation.

In the text we see that Abigail "wasted no time" (1 Samuel 25:18a). Because she may have been faithful in past difficult situations, and she knew the God of her people, she immediately sprang to work. She didn't take a long time to mourn her predicament. Because of her God-given wisdom, she understood that this situation would escalate quickly unless she took action. Fear did not hold her back; it propelled her forward.

Her action was not merely for herself, however. We get the sense that she had a strong relationship with the household servants and longed to preserve their lives as well. Sometimes we cannot act merely for our own self-preservation; when we realize our actions will also benefit others, that helps us make bold choices.

Speak the truth in love.

Abigail did not sugarcoat her husband's sin when discussing him with David, and yet she fought to preserve his life. She told the truth about him, then intervened on his behalf by taking the responsibility upon herself and giving David gifts. We see this kind of identification repentance in other places in the Bible as well, as when Daniel and Nehemiah repented before God on behalf of their nation. Though they did not personally commit the idolatries, they confessed the sin to God and asked for forgiveness as if they had. In this sense, Abigail gives us a foretaste of the Messiah who would bear the sins he did not commit to save the lives of untold millions throughout time.

Similarly, we can speak the truth with love as our motive. We can choose to intervene in another's life—not dismissing their sin but acknowledging it.

Of course, this doesn't mean we are unwise. There are evil people in this world who are hellbent on our destruction and/or their own. There may come a time when speaking the truth in love means getting away from them so we can be safe and create strong boundaries. This is why we need the Holy Spirit; he helps us know when to intervene, when to speak, when not to speak, and when we need to protect ourselves. The fact that Abigail was in an extremely hard marriage doesn't mean all women today must remain in destructive marriages. In fact, God loves women, and he wants them to be safe from harm.

Humble yourself.

Abigail did not presume upon David's kindness. Instead, she humbled herself before him, appealing to his powerful position and better nature. When we are overlooked, and particularly when we're afraid, we tend to shift into self-preservation mode. This centers our attention on ourselves, and it makes us desperate. But Abigail maintained her dignity even in humility, and God honored her for it. She emulated 1 Peter 5:6–7:

> So humble yourselves under the mighty power of God, and at the right time he will lift you up in honor. Give all your worries and cares to God, for he cares about you.

Know your Bible.

Abigail didn't know she was living through major historical events, but she did know God's exploits through David. She mentions this in 1 Samuel 25:29 when she tells David she knows he's been chased by Saul. She speaks of a "treasure pouch"—referencing the pouch in which he had carried five smooth stones when he faced Goliath as a young man. She further emphasizes his victory over Goliath in saying, "But the lives of your enemies will disappear like stones shot from a sling!"

Similarly, when we are overlooked, we can turn to the pages of the Bible to remind ourselves of God's ability to act on behalf of the unseen. Knowing the Word of God helps us navigate desperate situations. While our emotions may fluctuate, his Word is a rock in the sea of stress.

Let God defend you.

In intervening to save Nabal's life, Abigail relegated herself to an uncertain future. But God defended her from Nabal's retaliation.

When we are unnoticed, it's tempting to do everything we can to make sure every person in our life knows our side of the story. We can be tempted to become our own PR managers. Personally, I've had to remind myself that God's understanding of the complicated situation is exponentially more astute than mine. Therefore, he knows best how to defend me and will fight on my behalf. It is never easy to relinquish those reins of control, but Abigail did, then waited for her deliverance—one wrought through Nabal's death and David's kindness. In short, she trusted God's timing.

Abigail experienced much trauma—married to a hostile man, then living an itinerant life as one of David's wives before his coronation. She had to live in Philistine territory, then suffer a frightening kidnapping in which she must have feared she would be sexually assaulted and possibly killed. And yet, she shines as an example of someone who trusted the God who Sees.

Truths about Untrapped You

- Even in the direst circumstances, the Lord takes note of your suffering.
- When life gets difficult, the Scriptures can remind you of God's faithfulness through history.
- Treating others with kindness and respect is your superpower.
- How you treat others influences how you endure trials.

Questions for Discussion

1. What kind of emotions did the story of Abigail, Nabal, and David bring up for you? Why?
2. What does Abigail's rapid intervention teach you about hearing and obeying God?
3. When have you felt like Abigail? What relationship has been hard for you to live through or talk about? Do you have a friend who is walking through a difficult marriage?
4. Why do you think David relented from destroying Nabal?
5. What does Abigail's story teach you about faithfulness?

CHAPTER SIX

Jehosheba, the Unseen One

The kingdom of Israel had been shattered in two, violently divided with Israel to the north and Judah to the south. Princess Jehosheba felt the division in her heart, as if the tearing of the kingdom had wrenched her soul in two. As an unsevered kingdom under David, then his son Solomon, Israel had thrived. But Solomon's son, Rehoboam, had inaugurated disunity, strife, and the nation ultimately split amid a dispute over taxation.

With both her husband and her son now in the grave, Athaliah sought to cement her own rule . . . by murdering the grandchildren who would inherit the throne by right.

Although Athaliah also was a descendant of David, Jehosheba knew she considered such things a terrible inconvenience. She was obsessed only with power in the here and now and never could see beyond her own reign.

That is what quickened Jehosheba's heart and was the subject of her hurried conversations with Jehoiada, her priest-husband. They knew the laws of God. They understood the preciousness of life, that the image of Yahweh rested upon all. And they knew David to be a man after the heart of God himself—and that his family line must be preserved. Jehosheba had a prophetic view of the world; she knew she did not exist in this epoch of time only, but that what she did today would matter to future generations. Once a line of kings is decimated, it is lost forever.

She paced the upper roof of her home, wringing her hands. "What are we to do?"

"You know the Torah is clear. We must save lives, dear Jehosheba," Jehoiada said. He leaned forward on the parapet, looking out over Jerusalem, the Temple shining under a hot sun just to the north.

"But surely, she cannot kill her own grandchildren! What kind of witchcraft would inspire such a thing?" Jehosheba continued her pacing.

"The kind of heart that is darkened at the root," her husband said. He took a long drink from an earthen jar.

"You know the implications, don't you?"

"That we will be risking our lives?" He handed her the water jug.

She drank, trying to steady herself. Was she willing to die? Could she risk it all? "It is as you say, but I must think of the future. To think only of myself and the day is to disown the tenets of God, to forget the promises he made to this nation through Father Abraham." She stopped pacing, then faced the Temple.

"It has to be there." He pointed in the direction of her gaze. "It's the only safe place."

"But how?"

"They're housed separately, so you can't reach them all. If you try to rescue one of the older ones—"

"They are nieces and nephews, Jehoiada. They are not unconnected to me."

"Yes, I know, but what I meant is this: We must be careful. If the rumors are true, then she aims to kill them all. If you try to kidnap one of the older nephews, he will yell, and you will—"

She sat upon the ledge, the air in her lungs feeling hot and heavy. "Yes, if someone yells, I will be immediately found out."

"You'll lose them and yourself." He knelt before her, touched her cheek, then kissed it. "It must be Joash, the baby. You can conceal him more easily, and perhaps he will not cry."

They said nothing more as the sun retreated toward the great sea.

Jehosheba removed her sandals, then silently padded down the corridor of the queen's residence. She couldn't bear to think of the carnage the queen would soon enact. Her nephews. Her nieces. But she couldn't concern herself with the many. God had called her to the one, the baby whose name meant "given by the Lord."

Kidnapping itself was its own crime, she knew. The Torah was quite clear on the matter: "If anyone kidnaps a fellow Israelite and treats him as a slave or sells him, the kidnapper must die." She remembered the words Jehoiada had quoted to her last night. But she would not be treating baby Joash as a slave. And she certainly would not sell him. She was trying to save his life.

At the nursery entrance, she pulled in a breath and said a prayer. *Dear God, please let the baby be asleep.*

But when she walked through the doorway, a woman stood there. Joash's nurse! What would she do?

She rushed to Joash, scooped the sleeping boy into her arms

(*Thank God!*), and whispered to his nurse, "Hurry, you must come with me. The queen aims to kill him and all his siblings today."

Miraculously, the nurse didn't ask questions or hesitate. Together they spirited the baby away to an inner room of the mighty Temple where he would be safe from the mad queen's rampage.

Thankfully, the queen must have hired out the murdering work and thought the task complete because she never did a nationwide search for the missing boy. She either assumed her orders were obeyed, or her hired men didn't accurately report the death toll. Jehosheba, slowly, let out her breath.

Seven years later.

In the seventh year after Queen Athaliah stole the throne of Judah, Jehoiada summoned five stalwart army commanders of the Judean army to the Temple. Each arrived clandestinely at night, careful to avoid the others. And then he secretly summoned all the Levites and all Judah's clan leaders to the Temple as well.

Once everyone had gathered, Jehosheba summoned seven-year-old Joash. She placed her hand upon his head while tears ran down her cheeks. She had grown fond of her young nephew and worried for his safety, even if everything went as planned.

Jehoiada gathered all the subversives, then pointed to the boy. "Here is the king's son!" he declared. "The time has come for him to reign!"

With this, a roar of applause and shouting rose from the men. At first Jehosheba feared their outcry, but then she realized they were in the bowels of the Temple and the queen, far away in her palace, couldn't hear them. They could cheer.

"The Lord has promised that a descendant of David will be our king!"

Another joyful shout echoed off the Temple's stone walls.

Jehosheba bent low and whispered in Joash's ear, "All will be well, young prince. Soon you will be king."

Jehoiada motioned for the crowd to quiet down. "This is what you must do." He looked at the priests to his right. "When you priests and Levites come on duty on the Sabbath, a third of you will serve as gatekeepers." He pointed toward the palace south of them. "Another third will go over to the royal palace, and the final third of you will be at the Foundation Gate." He motioned toward the rest of the crowd. "Everyone else should stay in the courtyards of the Lord's Temple."

A murmur passed through the crowd.

"Remember," he said, "only the priests and Levites on duty may enter the Temple of the Lord, for they are set apart as holy. The rest of the people must obey the Lord's instructions and stay outside. You Levites form a bodyguard around the king and keep your weapons in hand." He gathered the Levites closer, then lowered his voice. "Kill anyone who tries to enter the Temple. Stay with the king wherever he goes."

As they waited for the Sabbath to dawn, Jehosheba counseled her young nephew, pouring into him the last bits of everything she knew of the Lord. Her husband had educated him thoroughly—a Davidic king must know the Law, after all.

When the Sabbath came, all those Jehoiada had instructed did exactly as he said, which calmed Jehosheba. Perhaps today Joash could step into his destiny?

Jehoiada outfitted the commanders with shields that used to be King David's and spears that had been stored in the Temple's belly. *Fitting*, Jehosheba thought.

At the priest's command, the people formed a circle around the Temple, with Joash and the altar at the center. Jehoiada placed the royal crown upon the boy's head and the priests presented Joash with the text of God's laws. They anointed him with the sacred oil, then proclaimed him king.

Four words rose as a powerful declaration from the crowds surrounding the boy.

"Long live the king! Long live the king! Long live the king!"

Jehosheba listened as the chant grew in intensity, flowing from their inner circle in the Temple to the crowds of people outside.

Jehoiada escorted the new king to his place of authority by the pillar at the Temple's entrance, surrounded by guards. Trumpeters joined the revelry. More people poured in from the surrounding area and added their musical instruments to the merriment. Songs spontaneously erupted from the crowd—and dancing, too.

As the cacophony reached a fever pitch, Queen Athaliah approached the Temple. Jehosheba had never seen her so pale, nor her eyes defeated like that. Amid the shouting, praising, and singing, she ripped her beautiful gown and screamed, "Treason! Treason!"

But Jehoiada would not allow her to make any speeches. He ordered the military commanders to take the screeching woman out of the Temple. "Kill anyone who tries to rescue her," he said as they dragged her away toward the palace.

They killed Queen Athaliah at the Horse Gate on the palace grounds.

Thus began the forty-year era of reform. Jehosheba was proud of her husband, who renewed Judah's commitment to their Lord. Together, the citizens solemnly vowed that they would be the Lord's people from that point forward. And they renewed the covenant between the king and his people.

Soon after, all the people—not just the priests!—ventured to the temple of Baal and destroyed it completely. The altars were desecrated, the idols crushed, and its high priest was killed.

The people returned to the ways of David. Jehoiada wanted to further protect the Temple, so he employed guards to watch over it. Once all this was accomplished, the guards, the commanders, and the people of Judah escorted King Joash from the Temple with much fanfare to the palace where his evil matriarch had once reigned.

Once again, Judah experienced the *shalom* of God. Not only had God protected all of them, but he kept his promise to preserve the line of King David. This brought Jehosheba much joy.

The Biblical Narrative

The story of Jehosheba is found in 2 Kings 11 and 2 Chronicles 22–23:15. Some have called it "a biblical Game of Thrones."[1] *Jehosheba* means "fullness or oath of the Lord." And this woman lived up to her name! Her determination to save a descendant of David preserved the family line that eventually produced Jesus Christ.

Although Joash is not mentioned by name in the Matthew 1 genealogy, his grandfather Jehoram and his grandson Uzziah are. (See Matthew 1:8–9.) Historians are unclear whether Athaliah is Jehosheba's mother or stepmother; I chose to portray her as "the evil stepmother" because that made the most sense to me. In that time, men could have several wives, as well as concubines; Jehosheba's mother easily could have been one of them.

How This Applies to Unseen You

What can we learn from Jehosheba's gutsy actions?

Being unseen can be a blessing in disguise.

It's interesting to note that the queen, Athaliah, did not suspect Jehosheba of doing anything, simply because she overlooked her as a potential subversive. In this case, being unnoticed proved to be a shield. And that has implications for us.

When in my teens, I was a new Christian still sporting a deep father wound. Understandably, I longed for a boyfriend—someone to tell me I would be OK, someone to hug and acknowledge me. But despite my prayers, boys constantly overlooked me, much to my bewilderment. In retrospect, I am utterly grateful for that fact, because I probably would have made an idol of anyone paying me any attention.

Similarly, when I started writing in 2005, I longed to be noticed in the literary world. I wanted readers to see me, to buy my books, to help me become a bestselling author. That did not happen—ever. I have been a solidly midlist author my entire career. At first, I railed against that fact, mourned it, and wondered why this elusive dream remained out of reach, but now I understand. Had I been noticed then, my ego would've blossomed, and not in the right way. God preserved my soul by limiting my success. My overlookedness had a positive impact on me.

Although it's speculation on my part (since it's not mentioned in the ancient text) that Jehosheba was unnoticed, it makes logical sense that it would help her carry out her plan. Perhaps it's a good exercise for us all to see how being overlooked has led to better things.

Your past does not predict your future.

Jehosheba grew up in a very dysfunctional family, with maniacal grandparents (Ahab and Jezebel). And yet she did not turn out like them. Instead of worshiping the common idol of the time, Baal, she married Judah's high priest. From the text we can surmise that Jehoiada was a righteous man who longed to see his nation return to its better roots. Together, he and Jehosheba found a new way forward for her family and their entire nation. This is good news for us! Though we may have grown up around difficult people who worship anything other than God, that does not mean we have to turn out that way. The intersection of God's loyal love and our obedience changes everything. Though it is not easy to walk away from past patterns, it is possible with God's help. Jehosheba not only defied the conventions of her family but ministered in the opposite spirit. Athaliah wanted death; Jehosheba chased life. Athaliah was cruel; Jehosheba protected an infant. What a beautiful reversal, from dysfunction to function!

We can become part of God's story simply by saying yes.

Jehosheba didn't know how her story would ultimately turn out. She simply did the right thing at the right time. But her actions had repercussions for centuries—even to this day. By preserving the line of David, through which the Messiah would come, she impacted you and me. Don't underestimate the power of a small act of obedience. You may not even understand its implications, but with the dynamic of God's Kingdom math, that small yes could lead to an exponential number of yeses in the future. Paul affirms this when he writes, "For all of God's promises have been fulfilled in Christ with a resounding 'Yes!' And through Christ, our 'Amen' (which means 'Yes') ascends to God for his glory" (2 Corinthians 1:20). Jehosheba's life illustrates the power of simple obedience.

We must obey God over anyone else.

The unnoticed Jehosheba did not conform to her family's ways because she had a much higher loyalty—to the God of her ancestors. In taking baby Joash, she revealed that she feared God in holy reverence and cherished his promises for the Messiah far more than she valued her very life. The truth is that sometimes God will call you to that higher allegiance, and your act of obedience for him will cause other people—even your own family—to hate you. Jesus reminded us of this when he warned:

> "Don't imagine that I came to bring peace to the earth! I came not to bring peace, but a sword. 'I have come to set a man against his father, a daughter against her mother, and a daughter-in-law against her mother-in-law. Your enemies will be right in your own household!'" (Matthew 10:34–36)

In the second part of this verse, Jesus is quoting Micah 7:6. Following God may mean quietly defying your family. Why? Because the Kingdom of God is opposed to the kingdom of darkness, and sometimes our family members reside in the latter. The question is: Will we choose to obey God, no matter the cost? Jehosheba chose God's way, but it could have cost her life. That's radical obedience. It demonstrates who she revered most.

The rarely exegeted story of Jehosheba reminds us that the unnoticed women of the Bible actually had great impact. In her case, it meant the preservation of the Messiah's line—no small feat. When you feel overlooked or unseen, remember her grit in doing the right thing.

Truths about Seen You

- God empowers you to preserve life and to do what is right.
- God uses a community to rescue others.
- You can, through the power of God, do what seems impossible.
- When you step in to prevent evil, you are doing the work of God.
- It's important to see that those who will come after you matter and that your legacy is important.

Questions for Discussion

1. Have you ever known you had to intervene in a situation but that the consequences for doing so might be troublesome? What did you do?
2. In today's world, who are the people most at risk? What can be done for them?
3. What did you know about Jehosheba before reading this account? What surprised you?
4. How do you think Jehosheba's marriage to a priest in the Lord's Temple influenced her actions?
5. What does the story of Jehosheba teach you about obeying the Lord no matter what?

CHAPTER SEVEN

Anna, the Unacknowledged One

Anna looked at her gnarled hands, then thanked the Almighty that they could still grasp water jars and touch the face of a needy friend. Every wrinkle, every age spot, every odd bend of the finger told its own story—of her life, loss, and life after loss.

She boiled water, then steeped lavender inside, adding honey and a squeeze of lemon—a tonic meant to keep her alert. Lately, her need to nap had extended even through her prayer times. *The body is just a receptacle for the soul*, she thought, but lately, at age eighty-four, hers had felt like a dried-up wineskin, bereft of flexibility.

Anna groaned as she rose from her spot beside the bed in the tiny room adjacent to the mighty Temple. The leaders had taken seriously Yahweh's mandate to care for widows and had provided the room for her in their benevolence. She paid them back in prayers. Her ancient knees had worn divots in the rock floor, proof of her labor for her people. Hours she would spend interceding, asking God for healing, restoration, and light.

As she sat upon her bed, she hollered heavenward, "You said it would happen—before my death. Well, I'm getting closer, so when will it be?" Her questions echoed off the stone walls. God did not answer her back. She chided herself for the spells of doubt—which came more frequently now as her fatigue deepened.

She closed her eyes, remembering the precise moment. Had it all been a dream? Wishful thinking? No. It had been as solid as the cool stone beneath her feet.

The events of Anna's life had turned on three hinges: her marriage to Nathan when she was eighteen, his sudden death seven years later, and the vision God had given her when she was sixty-five. She had been like Moses in the waiting, with forty years between Nathan's demise and the vision. She wondered how many more years she might have to wander and wonder before seeing it fulfilled.

At sixty-five her physical eyesight had been keener, and her spiritual eyes were finally adjusting to the realities of the Kingdom of God. That, she knew, was her crossover year between sight and insight. It was also the year her father, Phanuel from Asher's tribe, had breathed his last. His hand, she remembered, had resembled the way hers looked today. She spent days turned to nights at his bedside, praying and asking God for mercy. Phanuel had pulled in ragged breaths until he began sipping them, siphoning the smallest amount of air into his faintly rising chest, panting. She willed her own breath into his lungs, but he continued to struggle.

Day and night morphed into a phantasmagoric state of wake-sleep as her father clutched at life. She sang the *Shema* over him, reminding him of the welcoming feast Mother would have prepared when he passed over, and spoke of the faithfulness of Yahweh through all the stories of their people. She repeated them back to him; he had sown them into her heart, and now she returned the favor.

When she spoke of the Passover, the vision erupted before her: Light illuminated the dank room that had been paling in the pallor of death. Before her stood a man, taller than Goliath of old, clothed in starlight. He said no words, but she understood at once what he communicated with her. There would be One who would, once and for all, rescue his people. He would be their deliverer, and she would meet him before she died. He would not come as a king, but as an infant. She tried to ask how she would know the identity of the child, but there was no answer.

The light dissipated like mist upon a lake, leaving her alone with her father again—only this time, his face had grayed, and his sunken chest had stopped rising. He had gone to sleep with their forefathers, and Anna felt the weight of his loss. She had no children, no husband, no sisters, no brothers—only the Lord God Almighty.

For nineteen years, she had fed on that internal knowing of the Messiah Child she would one day meet. She listened intently to the rabbis, purposing to understand the promises of God in her era. She memorized large portions of the Torah and puzzled over God's promise to Abram—that he would be a father of many nations, not merely his own. The whole cosmos would be blessed by the God of Abraham—every tribe, tongue, and nation. But her own nation had struggled to obey Yahweh. They had been enslaved, freed, and then wandered before entering the Promised Land. They had chased after idols, endured Babylonian exile, and then miraculously returned to their homeland. But centuries had passed between that time and today.

"How long, O Lord?" she asked.

Silence welcomed her, as it always did.

This was the life of a prophetess, she knew; the messages God dropped into her mind were infrequent. But when they came, she obeyed the inkling and shared them freely. The greatest joy in her life came at two points now: when she heard the voice of the Almighty and when she conveyed his encouragement to one of his people.

There were gaps of waiting, though. Long stretches of silence.

Still, she prayed. Still, she worshiped—at all hours, morning, midday, and evening. Still, she fasted, waiting for this promised deliverer. She wanted to make sure she was so close to God that she would not miss such a beautiful sight. Surely God would show her, right? The Messiah would not pass her by.

As usual, she pulled on her head covering and exited her home in the Temple's bowels. She made her way to the spot where the purification ceremony took place, where faithful people of God dedicated their firstborn sons. She shaded her eyes from the light, breathing heavily as she padded closer. Her feet ached. She prayed for strength.

Ahead of her, an older man was holding a baby while a couple presented two turtledoves to the priest. This had been the way of things ever since she started attending these ceremonies—but today, something felt charged, as if the air around her buzzed like a beehive. *Could it be. . . ?*

As she drew closer, she noticed the man holding the baby, but she could not quite make out who he was. She asked the attendant next to her, "Who is holding that baby?"

"Simeon," the man said.

She'd heard of Simeon but had never met him. He'd been known to share something beautifully similar to her vision—a message about a Messiah coming to Israel. She had never sought him out, but knowing he'd heard a similar message from God in the past thrilled her. Though she never shared her vision publicly, she knew she was not alone. When God was going to move in miraculous ways, he would make them known, just as he had for Moses and Aaron before parting the Red Sea.

At that moment, Simeon found his voice. Anna drew closer.

Now she could see the wrinkles in the creases of his eyes, the smile upon his face, the glee in his countenance. "Sovereign Lord," Simeon said, "Now let your servant die in peace, as you have promised."

Could it be?

"I have seen your salvation," he trilled, "which you have prepared for all people. He is a light to reveal God to the nations, and he is the glory of your people Israel!"

Anna noticed the surprised looks of the baby's parents. And in her heart, she knew: This was the Awaited One.

Simeon blessed the baby boy and his parents. He turned to the boy's mother and said, "This child is destined to cause many in Israel to fall, and many others to rise. He has been sent as a sign from God, but many will oppose him."

What kind of deliverer would this be? Why wouldn't his own people welcome him? Anna thought.

With tears rolling down his aged cheek, Simeon touched the mother's upper arm and said, "As a result, the deepest thoughts of many hearts will be revealed. And a sword will pierce your very soul."

The mother looked startled—and so did Anna. Simeon's words that had begun so beautifully about salvation and light turned quickly to misunderstanding and soul piercing. This deliverer would suffer, as would those close to him. And yet, who was she to question God's ways? He was a God who surprised. A God who worked in mysterious ways. A God of nuance and power and beauty. This swaddled baby would rescue a sin-darkened world, she felt it. He would be its savior.

From within her spirit, Anna suddenly burst into praise and song. Nineteen years of waiting crashed over her in waves. She thought of Elijah, then, after God's powerful display against the prophets of Baal, how the people had yelled, "The Lord—he is God! The Lord—he is God!" She drew near to the child, glimpsing his rosy cheeks, noting his almond eyes, strong nose, and perfect mouth. A shock of dark brown hair covered his head, and he seemed to smile under her gaze. *This is him*, she felt God say. *This is my Son.*

Later, the memory of that moment stayed with her as she sought people who had the same hope for Israel's rescue. She found pockets of community around the Temple's gates who were waiting expectantly for God to intervene in Jerusalem. With these, she shared her story, encouraging them that God had heard their prayers. He had sent a Messiah; they had received an indescribable gift.

She continued to pray, knees deep in the divots of her little home. She continued to worship and fast. She taught the ways of God to people whenever she could—that he would not come as expected, but perhaps in disguise. Their task was to have open hearts, ready to receive him. "I have seen the Lord," she said. "And he was a baby, dedicated at eight days old." She marveled at the kindness of God to sustain her through her widowhood, entrust her with prophetic messages, and bless her with a glimpse of heaven before her death.

Though her body was decaying, her heart soared ever higher, as if her soul flourished while her limbs weakened. Her sight, dimmer than ever, represented her soul's opposite. She could now see clearly, and this sight prepared her for glory.

The Biblical Narrative

Anna the prophetess from Luke 2:26–28 was a long-term widow. As I penned her story, I took some liberty with it, giving her a vision much like the one Simeon had—about the Messiah coming in her lifetime. I did this because she was a prophetess; God spoke to her, and it made sense that she had been prepared for that beautiful moment in the Temple. Another powerful truth: Since the time of Malachi—the last minor prophet in the Old Testament—no prophet had arisen in Israel. And yet, the Apostle Luke names Anna as a prophetess in his gospel account. By contrast, Simeon gave a prophetic declaration at Jesus's dedication, but he was not called a prophet. The fact that Anna was declared a prophetess revealed that God was doing something in their midst! It would remind the people of God of the words of the prophet Joel:

> "Then, after doing all those things, I will pour out my Spirit upon all people. Your sons and daughters will prophesy. Your old men will dream dreams, and your young men will see visions." (Joel 2:28)

This is a signpost—an alert for God's people. It's as if the Lord is shouting in this scene: "Watch this! Take note! The Kingdom of God is manifesting before your very eyes!" Of course, we know the fulfillment of these verses came later, when God poured out his Spirit on the disciples in the upper room (recorded in Acts 2). Anna was an example of what was to come; her life was a prophecy for us!

Phanuel (Anna's father) means "face of God." *Anna* means "favor or grace."[1] Anna's life may not have made her feel very favored, though; she had lived for so long as a widow, tucked away in the Temple without a husband's companionship. No little girl grows up hoping to be widowed young, or to remain that way into her eighties.

Anna's office of prophetess is not common in the Bible, but it's also not unheard of. We already studied Miriam and Deborah, who both held that title. Huldah the wife of Shallum, Isaiah's wife, and Philip's four unmarried daughters (mentioned in Acts 21:9) also prophesied. A case can be made for Elizabeth as well.

In looking at the scene with Simeon, Mary, Joseph, and baby Jesus, it's important to look back to what God required of each of them. First, according to the Abrahamic Covenant, all boys were to be circumcised on their eighth day of life.

> "This is the covenant that you and your descendants must keep: Each male among you must be circumcised. You must cut off the flesh of your foreskin as a sign of the covenant between me and you. From generation to generation, every male child must be circumcised on the eighth day after his birth." (Genesis 17:10–12)

Luke tells us how this happened for Jesus:

> Eight days later, when the baby was circumcised, he was named Jesus, the name given him by the angel even before he was conceived. (Luke 2:21)

This circumcision most likely took place in Bethlehem, though the Scripture is silent on that point.

I used to read this passage as if it were one event: Jesus being circumcised, then instantly meeting Simeon and Anna at his dedication. But Mary followed the laws of purification, so it would have been the fortieth day when she and Joseph took Jesus to the Temple.

God commanded his people to dedicate the firstborn of their families and even their livestock before they crossed over from Egypt through the Red Sea: "Dedicate to me every firstborn among the Israelites. The first offspring to be born, of both humans and animals, belongs to me" (Exodus 13:1). There are more specifics in Leviticus 12:4 about a woman being ritually unclean for seven days after giving birth to a child—and if the child is a boy, she must remain isolated for an additional thirty-three days to "be purified from the bleeding of childbirth. During this time of purification, she must not touch anything that is set apart as holy. And she must not enter the sanctuary until her time of purification is over." Once the woman has been purified, she is to bring an offering to the Temple.

It's interesting to note that Joseph accompanied Mary on that mission. According to the Law, she was to bring a one-year-old lamb for a burnt offering and a young pigeon or turtledove as a purification offering, presenting them to a priest at the Temple's entrance. God also made provisions for the poor here:

> "If a woman cannot afford to bring a lamb, she must bring two turtledoves or two young pigeons. One will be for the burnt offering and the other for the purification offering." (Leviticus 12:8)

By offering birds (see Luke 2:24), we see that Mary and Joseph are poor. Here's the beautiful part though: *They* did *bring a lamb!* As John the Baptist said, Jesus was "the Lamb of God who takes away the sin of the world!" (John 1:29).

How This Applies to Unacknowledged You

What else do we learn about Anna in this short passage in Luke? Here's the exact verbiage:

> Anna, a prophet, was also there in the Temple. She was the daughter of Phanuel from the tribe of Asher, and she

> was very old. Her husband died when they had been married only seven years. Then she lived as a widow to the age of eighty-four. She never left the Temple, but stayed there day and night, worshipping God with fasting and prayer. She came along just as Simeon was talking with Mary and Joseph, and she began praising God. She talked about the child to everyone who had been waiting expectantly for God to rescue Jerusalem. (Luke 2:36–38)

As mentioned before, Anna is a widow. She represents one aspect of the quartet of the vulnerable (widow, orphan, alien, poor) that God instructed Israel to honor and care for. We see all four in this minor prophet's admonition:

> "This is what the Lord of heaven's Armies says: Judge fairly and show mercy and kindness to one another. Do not oppress widows, orphans, foreigners, and the poor. And do not scheme against each other." (Zechariah 7:9–10)

Perhaps this is why she is given housing in or near the Temple. It was common to overlook vulnerable people, but Israel was called to a higher standard. It's interesting to note that the sin we commonly hold against Sodom and Gomorrah is not the indictment God gives later: "Sodom's sins were pride, gluttony, and laziness, while the poor and needy suffered outside her door" (Ezekiel 16:49). God is displeased with people who abuse the vulnerable.

Certainly, Jesus noticed widows when he walked the earth. When a poor woman put two small coins in the Temple offering, he said,

> "This poor widow has given more than all the rest of them. For they have given a tiny part of their surplus, but she, poor as she is, has given everything she has." (Luke 21:3–4)

(Aside: wouldn't it be compelling if this widow had been Anna? Though that would make her well over 100 years old.) This idea of caring for the vulnerable is carried into the New Covenant. James writes, "Pure and genuine religion in the sight of God the Father means caring for orphans and widows in their distress and refusing to let the world corrupt you" (1:27). In this, we can see there is an odd benefit to being overlooked: When everyone overlooks a broken person, God fights on his or her behalf.

Before we move on, we must explore what life was like for a widow in the time after Christ's resurrection, as well as how the church was instructed to care for them. As in ancient times, widows had little protection. In a patriarchal society, all provision for women came through marriage and a husband. To lose a husband was not only to lose a companion but meant loss of economic stability. That is why it was up to the community to provide for widows. If the community did not, that widow could die.

In his first letter to Timothy, the Apostle Paul writes:

> Take care of any widow who has no one else to care for her. But if she has children or grandchildren, their first responsibility is to show godliness at home and repay their parents by taking care of them. This is something that pleases God. Now a true widow, a woman who is truly alone in this world, has placed her hope in God. She prays night and day, asking God for his help. But the widow who lives only for pleasure is spiritually dead

> even while she lives. Give these instructions to the church so that no one will be open to criticism. . . . A widow who is put on the list for support must be a woman who is at least sixty years old and was faithful to her husband. She must be well respected by everyone because of the good she has done. Has she brought up her children well? Has she been kind to strangers and served other believers humbly? Has she helped those who are in trouble? Has she always been ready to do good? (1 Timothy 5:3–7, 9–10)

Anna did not live long enough to see the church emerge, but she did embody many of the traits Paul encouraged: She was over sixty. She had been married for seven years. She was well respected. She did good. She spent her time in prayer and fasting. She was a strong example to anyone whose station in life is precarious. Widowhood did not prevent her from living generously.

Here are several more things we can learn from Anna's example.

God uses unnoticed people (perhaps more than he uses the noticed ones!).

Jesus often noticed the unnoticed when he walked the earth. He dignified the woman at the well, protected the woman caught in adultery, healed the lepers, and called Zaccheus out of a tree to his side. His life didn't result in a military coup or a supernatural take-over of Rome; his ways were unexpected, but they revealed the very nature of God, who loves the broken. In fact, it's the marginalized who most recognize their need for him and, in that recognition, experience his strength—perhaps more than those who feel noticed by the world. The Apostle Paul puts this eloquently in his first letter to the Corinthian church:

> Remember, dear brothers and sisters, that few of you were wise in the world's eyes or powerful or wealthy when God called you. Instead, God chose things the world considers foolish in order to shame those who think they are wise. And he chose things that are powerless to shame those who are powerful. God chose things despised by the world, things counted as nothing at all, and used them to bring to nothing what the world considers important. As a result, no one can ever boast in the presence of God. (1 Corinthians 1:26–29)

This is the beauty of God's great, upside-down Kingdom. Those who are overlooked are noticed. Those who are poor are made rich (in Christ). Those who have no power are given the ability to endure. When you feel overlooked, instead of lamenting, stop yourself. This is a place of great privilege! When you see your lack, you're in a better position to experience the strength God provides.

Age does not disqualify you from pursuing the things of God.

Some scholars believed Anna to be much older than the eighty-four years I've given her here, saying that she *had been a widow* for eighty-four years. The NET Bible notes this: "The chronology of the eighty-four years is unclear, since the final phrase could mean 'she was widowed until the age of eighty-four.'"[2] However, the more natural way to understand the term is as a reference to the length of her widowhood, in which case Anna would be about 105 years old.[3] If that's the case, she certainly had very little time on earth. And yet God allowed her not only to see the Messiah, but to perceive him correctly.

We live in an age of ageism. Whereas cultures around the world once honored their elders, ours idolizes youth. Instead of seeking out the counsel of the wise, we run to the foolishness of the young. This is backward, and it is wrong. The older saints in any congregation are its greatest treasures, but they are often relegated to performing only menial tasks or are ignored altogether. Church, sadly, has become utilitarian and corporate; it should not be a place of retirement, but of honor, where all the members work together toward a common mission.

Anna's story proves that there is no age limit on experiencing the presence and purpose of God. The world may shout otherwise, but the Lord is never finished with his saints.

One of my favorite podcasts is *Ask N. T. Wright Anything*. As I write this book, Dr. Wright is seventy-four years old, and he is a wealth of theological knowledge. He has pastored for many years in England and has written many theological books. My life is richer because of his scholarship. He is an example of God using a Christ-follower well past retirement age.

God's timing is spectacular.

Luke 2:38 says, "She came along just as Simeon was talking with Mary and Joseph, and began praising God." This was no coincidence. At the precise moment when Simeon was delivering his prophetic declaration, Anna the prophetess comes onto the scene, then rejoices. When we live a life of prayer, we have the privilege of experiencing God's surprising coincidences. And perhaps that's the beauty of an overlooked life—in that quiet place of spending time with God, with him being our all-in-all, we develop more receptivity to his ways. We become more sensitive to his timing and his promptings.

Gratitude is contagious.

Anna, who had little stature in the community (other than being known for her piety), didn't let her circumstances prevent her from sharing the good news. "She talked about the child to everyone who had been waiting expectantly for God to rescue Jerusalem" (Luke 2:38). Her gratitude overflowed to many. When we are overlooked, we tend to look at what we don't have. But Anna looked outside of herself—to the Lord. And this changed everything.

Perseverance matters.

The Greek in Luke 2 is instructive. *Ouk Aphistato* means "never left." *Ouk* is an absolute negation, meaning Anna literally never leaves the Temple. The verb *aphistato* is in the imperfect tense,[4] meaning it continues to happen daily, hourly. Anna continued to never leave the Temple, preferring to be with God where he was. She remained there always. If you think about the powerful fact that we are now God's temple, Anna's life (again!) became a signpost of what was to come. She embodied what we'd become—carriers of God in the temple of ourselves!

Anna spent her life looking forward, and that forward perspective kept her persevering. Similarly, as Christ's followers we are called to persevere while considering the heavenly hope in front of us. Having that as our aim, we are better able to exercise tenacity. Paul reminds us,

> Therefore, since God in his mercy has given us this new way, we never give up. We reject all shameful deeds and underhanded methods. We don't try to trick anyone or distort the word of God. We tell the truth before God, and all who are honest know this. . . . That is why we

> never give up. Though our bodies are dying, our spirits are being renewed every day. (2 Corinthians 4:1–2, 16)

Had Anna given up hope, she would not have seen the Lord. In her overlooked state as a widow, she knew she was seen by the only One who mattered. The compelling vision he gave her empowered her to keep looking for the Messiah.

Using the gifts God gives you reveals your faithfulness and brings glory to God.

We live in an age when splashy gifts are rewarded. We spend a lot of time analyzing ourselves, trying to discern how we tick, what our Enneagram type is, which strengths we possess, and what kinds of spiritual gifts we have. We pine for "important" traits. But God is not looking for gifted people who are noticed for their gifts; he is looking for faithful people who do what he says, often in small ways most people don't notice. (But, friend, he always notices!)

Jesus told the parable of the talents, in which a landowner gives three people some resources. Two double the investment, and one buries it. Jesus said this about the one who was given the most resources:

> "The servant to whom he had entrusted the five bags of silver came forward with five more and said, 'Master, you gave me five bags of silver to invest, and I have earned five more.' The master was full of praise. 'Well done, my good and faithful servant. You have been faithful in handling this small amount, so now I will give you many more responsibilities. Let's celebrate together!'" (Matthew 25:20–21)

We can use whatever the Lord has already given us. Anna had very little in the way of material possessions. Certainly, she had few resources. But she still practiced generosity. She fasted and prayed. She was known for her piety. Her faithfulness over a lifetime culminated in seeing Jesus Christ in the flesh!

Peter encourages us to use whatever giftings God has given us with all our strength. We are to be faithful.

> God has given each of you a gift from his great variety of spiritual gifts. Use them well to serve one another. Do you have the gift of speaking? Then speak as though God himself were speaking through you. Do you have the gift of helping others? Do it with all the strength and energy that God supplies. Then everything you do will bring glory to God through Jesus Christ. All glory and power to him forever and ever! Amen. (1 Peter 4:10–11)

Note that Peter admonishes these gifts are for the glory of Christ, not the one exercising the gift.

If you are a widow, your life is not over. If you feel too old to matter, God is not finished with you. It's never too late to pray, to give, to help, or to serve. Consider the state of feeling unacknowledged as an invitation to an adventurous life of prayer. You are the apple of God's eye. He loves you. He sees your needs. His Kingdom doesn't bend toward the splashy, but the faithful.

Truths about Acknowledged You

- God's economy is not the same as the world's. Little becomes much in his capable hands, including the desires of your heart.
- Age is not a limitation in the Kingdom of God—in fact, it's a benefit.
- There is a secret place where those who are broken go—a place where God speaks life over you.
- It's a joy to look beyond this life to the next, and it's valuable to leave a legacy of godliness behind.
- Your prayers are not pointless.

Questions for Discussion

1. How does knowing that God takes care of the quartet of the vulnerable help you understand his heart?
2. When you read the story of Simeon and Anna, did you discover something you hadn't seen before? If so, what was it?
3. Are there any widows in your life? How do you seek to bless them? If you are a widow, how has the body of Christ responded to you? How do you wish they would?
4. What have you been praying for the longest? How long have you been praying for it? Has God given you hints along the way or pinpricks of light to show you he's working behind the scenes?
5. What does the story of Anna teach you about perseverance?

CHAPTER EIGHT

Martha, the Hurried One

The small town of Bethany lay on the outskirts of the desert. It boasted good people and a conviviality that seemed to welcome the stranger, particularly since it was a village where pilgrims often stopped on their way to Jerusalem. Today was no different, though the fluttering of Martha's heart seemed to indicate a paradigm had shifted. She had heard of the man, Jesus of Nazareth—how he had healed the infirm, delivered the demonized, and talked to riffraff as though they were actual human beings with feelings. Together, she and her siblings, Lazarus and Mary, had spoken of him in hushed tones. Who was he, exactly? Was he the Messiah, as some had said? An imposter? A holy man? Someone who would finally emancipate them from Rome's endless tyranny?

Martha had been fascinated by stories of angels her whole life—how they suddenly appeared, made proclamations, and changed the trajectory of Israel's events. Would she someday meet one? She did not know, but she did know this: If she ever ran across one, she'd feed him, sure enough.

Mary ran into their small kitchen. "He is coming!"

"Who is coming?" Martha rolled the flatbread dough, wondering if it would rise better today than it had the last time. She willed the yeast to enliven it.

"Jesus of Nazareth!" Mary's eyes lit as she said the words.

Martha's stomach jumped within her. "Where?"

"I invited him to our home. And he is coming—with his companions. This very hour."

Mary might just as well have announced that Caiaphas the High Priest was coming to dinner. How could Martha possibly prepare something suitable for a man who scared demons? "When exactly?"

"I believe he is already here."

Martha meant to quickly tidy up before padding to the door, but there was no time. With each step she told herself to calm down. A peaceful house full of shalom would be a blessing to any weary stranger, she knew.

She opened the door. There stood an ordinary man of ordinary height with an ordinary beard. But his eyes? They were compelling, as if they looked through her right to her soul. "Welcome to our home," she stammered.

Jesus thanked her as he stepped into the room. Behind him followed twelve street-worn men, their musky scent wafting into the tiny Bethany residence. Thirteen men? And with her brother Lazarus, that made fourteen hearty appetites—plus Mary and Martha. How would she accommodate them all? Martha thanked the Almighty for the privilege of blessing the weary travelers and set about giving them water and a place to sit. She returned to the kitchen and prepared a lamb for roasting. Quickly, she slipped outside and baked the dough she'd been shaping in the well-heated oven. When it was done, the men ate every crumb as the lamb roasted. But there was still much more to do, so she scanned the room for Mary.

And there she was.

Jesus of Nazareth, breadless, taught the Torah like a good rabbi . . . and Mary sat at his feet like a rabbi's disciple—something no woman was allowed to be.

Scandalous! Who does she think she is, sitting at the foot of a rabbi? This position was solely reserved for men studying the Torah. Something stirred in Martha. Was it jealousy? Or was it incredulity at Mary's audacity? Or maybe she was just perplexed that a rabbi would allow such a display. Didn't he know the proper regulations for rabbis and pupils? Did he allow Mary to make an embarrassing display of herself in this way because he felt sorry for her? Was he just being kind? His face registered the shalom Martha longed for, as if propriety didn't matter to him at all. He seemed to exude joy over the fact that a student was absorbing his words, no matter what her sex.

The scent of roasting lamb brought Martha to her senses. She needed help. There was so much to cut and prepare and present! Martha knew she could not serve these men alone. She walked past the hungry disciples to address Jesus. *What should she call him? Rabbi?* But something within, perhaps the voice of the Almighty, prompted her: *Call him Lord.*

"Lord," she said.

Jesus looked at her and seemed to see her heart. A smile creased the corner of his eyes. He nodded—an invitation to continue.

She pointed to Mary, gazing up at Jesus's face. "Doesn't it seem unfair to you that my sister just sits here while I do all the work?" Her anger spilled out, but even as it did, she regretted it. It felt petty, particularly as Jesus exuded love her way. In a softer voice, she said, "Tell her to come and help me."

Jesus gazed into Mary's upturned face. A tear ran down his cheek, as if he were thanking Martha's kneeling sister. He turned to catch Martha's gaze again. "My dear Martha," he said, "you are worried and upset over all these details!"

Yes, I am. But I have cause.

He held her eyes. "There is only one thing worth being concerned about. Mary has discovered it, and it will not be taken away from her."

His words both cut and soothed Martha simultaneously. Mary looked at her, but she wasn't gloating. To the contrary, she seemed content, as if the world had spun off kilter only to be righted under the gaze of her new Lord.

Martha nodded. This interaction felt like a liturgy, something she would come back to many times in her life. It was a holy moment, she knew—the kind you tuck away until you're alone in the wilderness under a broad sky so you can replay it more clearly. It was true that she allowed overwhelming circumstances to crowd her thinking—but wasn't this true of everyone? Wouldn't anyone feel the same? But there was something in Jesus's words that held no scolding, only joy. His were words of friendship. And the correction at the end was prompted only by love.

Later, after the crowd of men had left their home fed and satisfied, Martha approached her sister on their rooftop. "The Rabbi . . ."

"Was he not compelling?" Mary asked.

"Indeed, he was." Martha paced the rooftop in the cool evening air. A star poked out of the dusky blue sky above.

"I am sorry," Mary said. "The moment he began teaching, I lost all sensibilities. You know how I long to see the Kingdom of God come here to earth? Well, he spoke of that, and he addressed me as if I were kin. He dignified my intelligence. He *saw* me."

"So, do you think he is the one we have been looking for? The awaited one?" Martha whispered. What if someone on a neighboring rooftop heard them? To talk of overthrowing Rome was treason.

"I do not yet know. But this I do know: He is unlike any man I have ever met."

They stood together, watching the stars make their entrance one by one.

A few minutes later, Lazarus joined them. He asked what they thought of Jesus and his disciples.

It was Martha who answered, "We must always, always welcome them whenever they're nearby. This will be our life's work, our one thing."

The friendship between Martha, Mary, Lazarus, and Jesus deepened as the rabbi continued to preach throughout the country. Whenever he and his disciples were nearby, they knew to stop in at the siblings' home for refreshment, conversation, and rest. Martha found profound joy in meeting all their needs. Whenever they stayed at the house, she made sure to donate some of her cached money to Judas, the treasurer of the group.

Together, they would all break bread while Jesus spoke of a new kingdom where the poor would be fed, the broken would be made whole, the outcast would be included, and the blind would see. Word of Jesus's exploits spread like a forest fire. He could silence a demon with a word, heal the leprous, and make the lame walk. Reports even came in of him raising a young girl from the dead. Crowds pressed in on him wherever he went, but when he came to their home, Martha could see he relaxed. He was among friends.

On one of his journeys through Israel, Jesus steered clear of

Jerusalem. Rumor was that the Sanhedrin had it out for him, that they were bent on destroying him. Many had warned him to stay away from that city because it was a hotbed of anger. And he had.

One afternoon as Martha prepared an evening meal, Mary rushed in.

"Come quickly," she said.

"What is it?" Martha wiped her hands on her dress, then adjusted her palla. She did not like the sound of alarm in Mary's voice. Had something happened to Jesus?

"Lazarus is very sick," Mary said. "Hurry!"

Martha followed Mary to Lazarus's side. He wore the sweat-soaked clothes he'd donned before working a day in the fields under the relentless sun. This wasn't unusual, but today, something was different. His hot brow screamed of fever. Martha dipped a cloth into their water pot, bringing it to his forehead. He shrank under her touch.

No matter what she and Mary did, the fever rose like the sun over Mount Hermon, except that it did not ebb into a sunset. It only grew angrier, more intense. Lazarus shifted from sanity to seeing demons. He cried out for Jesus, begging for relief.

By the next day, his condition had grown grave. He no longer would sip water, he labored to breathe, and his chest rattled. When he could speak, he gave the sisters instructions on what to do when he died.

Martha put a finger to his lips. "Save your strength. No need to tell us all this. You will recover." She shot a look her sister's way, then shifted her eyes as an invitation to leave the room.

Martha led Mary outside. "He is dying, Mary. You know it as well as I do. What are we to do?" She told herself not to cry, but tears gathered in her eyes anyway.

Mary wiped them away. "I need to tell Jesus. To heal our brother is a simple thing for him."

"Yes, you are right," Martha said. "Let's send a message to him. He loves Lazarus. Surely, he will change his plans and rush back."

They went inside, where Lazarus's breathing sounded like a death march. Martha wrote, "Lord, your dear friend is very sick" on a piece of papyrus. She rolled it up, sealed it with wax, then handed it to a young servant boy nearby who was swift of foot. She told him the approximate whereabouts of Jesus and his disciples and instructed him to hurry. A man's life was at stake.

The sisters waited. They prayed. They cried. They conferred with a local physician. But nothing changed, except that Lazarus continued to grow worse.

When the death rasp began, Martha recognized it. Their parents' lungs had rattled just like that before they took their last breaths. Though death was a reality in their lives, Martha hated it, hated that rattle—and hated that Jesus had not arrived to cure her brother.

Mary held one of Lazarus's hands and Martha the other as they held vigil next to his pallet on the floor of their home. Martha willed him to breathe, asking God to please give him her breath, but the Almighty would not answer her prayer. Each labored breath seemed to tire Lazarus more.

Mary brought water to his dried and cracking lips. "Please, you must drink." But the water only poured in rivulets through the crease of his lips down his jaw and into his ear. Martha wiped it away, as if that would change his state.

The sisters looked at each other over their brother's still-breathing form.

"It is time," Martha whispered. Lazarus's face had paled even more, and his breaths now came in horrid sips.

"No!" Mary cried. "The Lord will be here. Lazarus, he loves you. He will not forsake you. Please, please hang on."

At that, Lazarus drew in a breath, then looked at each sister. "All . . . will . . . be . . . well," he sputtered. He inhaled, then exhaled.

But he did not take another breath. The letting out of air had been his surrender to death, Martha knew.

"No!" Mary yelled. "No!"

Martha had very little left with which to comfort her sister. As she had done in the past, she internally instructed herself to keep going, to do the next right thing, and to attend to the funereal details of death. She closed Lazarus's eyes, which had stared, fixed, at the ceiling. She padded out of the room to make burial arrangements. It would not be long before her brother's body became a stench.

Martha kept looking for Jesus as they laid Lazarus in their family tomb. She expected him to come and comfort them—but he did not come. The servant boy had returned, told them that the message had been delivered, that Jesus had read it, but did not act on it. This small piece of information niggled at Martha's brain. Perhaps they weren't as close as she had thought? Maybe Jesus had more important matters to attend to? This had been a confusing point of conversation between her and Mary, and neither of them could make sense of it. *If Jesus loved Lazarus as he said he did, why did he not return in time?*

And if he truly loved them, why wouldn't he at least come to pay his respects at Lazarus's funeral?

Strong men rolled a large stone into place across the mouth of the cave that served as the family tomb. Martha heard it thud into its groove like an earthquake—a sound ending their happiness, their provision, and their future. Now what?

The mourners wailed alongside the sisters. Four days they remained as Lazarus rotted in the grave.

Still, there was no Jesus.

During the cacophony of wailing women (hired for such a grievous occasion), the young man said, "Jesus is coming."

Martha asked the women to quiet, then looked at Mary. "I'm going to him."

Mary said nothing. Her face registered nothing. She who had chosen "the one thing" could not bring herself to choose it again. She flicked her wrist Martha's way as if to say, *Go ahead. It won't matter.*

Martha ran down the road that led to their village. She scanned the countryside until her eyes landed on the familiar forms of a man and his disciples. *Jesus!*

Breathlessly, she met them on the roadway. For a moment she said nothing as the disciples backed away to give them space. "Lord," she said, "if only you had been here, my brother would not have died." She swallowed. "But even now I know that God will give you whatever you ask." She believed—but she also did not believe.

Jesus held her gaze, eyes moist. "Your brother will rise again," he said.

This, she knew. "Yes," she said, "he will rise when everyone else rises, at the last day." This brought her little solace, though—today's grief was thick and dark.

Jesus pointed to heaven, then to himself. "I am the resurrection and the life. Anyone who believes in me will live, even after dying. Everyone who lives in me and believes in me will never ever die."

The wind picked up, swirling dust around them. Martha shielded her eyes.

"Do you believe this, Martha?" Jesus asked.

Something indescribable welled up within her, but she could not ascertain what. Hope? Fear? "Yes, Lord," she said. "I have always believed you are the Messiah, the Son of God, the one who has come into the world from God."

Jesus embraced her and asked about Mary. So Martha returned to the house of mourning, found Mary, and said, "The Teacher is here and wants to see you."

Martha watched her sister walk down the dusty path. She squinted, rubbing the dust from her eyes as she watched Mary again fall to Jesus's feet, into the posture of a disciple. Martha did not know what transpired between them, but she saw Mary rise and the group begin walking toward the family tomb. Martha ran to meet them there.

The look on Jesus's face perplexed Martha. Tears stained it, but anger lived there too. She understood this intrinsically because her brother's death made her both angry and desperately sad. Could it be that the Messiah understood her plight? Would a Messiah weep?

The mourners still stood nearby, with the stone firmly in place. Lazarus was dead. Nothing could be done.

Martha embraced Mary. A holy hush fell over the crowd as they waited to see what Jesus would do. She felt she wanted to speak but could not. Something inside her told her to memorize this moment, to cherish it.

"Roll the stone aside," Jesus said.

Ever the practical one, Martha shot a look his way. "Lord, he has been dead for four days. The smell will be terrible."

The anger in Jesus's eyes turned to mild exasperation, as if his student had not retained obvious information. "Didn't I tell you that you would see God's glory if you believe?" he asked.

She said nothing; neither did Mary. They held hands.

Several of Jesus's disciples strained to roll the giant stone away from the tomb's entrance. Martha heard their grunts, then prepared herself for the stench.

Jesus looked to the sky. "Father," he said, "thank You for hearing me. You always hear me, but I said it out loud for the sake of all these people standing here, so that they will believe You sent me."

Why is he saying that? Martha grasped Mary's hand tighter. The sun seemed to spotlight the cave's entrance. No one spoke.

"Lazarus, come out!" Jesus's shout seemed to shake the earth. Martha had never heard him speak in such a way, full of authority.

At that moment, she turned toward the tomb. And there . . . could it be? Was it? *How?*

Lazarus, their beloved brother, stepped from the dank tomb, still shrouded in the grave clothes they had lovingly prepared for him. Mary screamed. Martha remained mute. Her mind could not process what she was seeing. *How could it be?* Eventually, she found her feet and ran with Mary to Lazarus's side. She wept. She laughed. She marveled at the miracle of resurrection.

"Unwrap him," Jesus said, "and let him go!"

The Biblical Narrative

We find the story of Martha throughout the gospels, particularly in Luke 10 and John 11 and 12. As we dive into the more overlooked of the three siblings (Martha), it's important to get some geography correct. Bethany, which means "house of figs," is a small village between Jerusalem and Jericho. Bethany is situated below the rise of the hill protecting the capital; you cannot see Jerusalem from there, so it feels like a secluded haven facing the famous Mount of Olives. In some ways, you could call the town a suburb of Jerusalem.

Bethany is also the town where Simon—a former leper whom

Jesus had healed—hosted a banquet in Jesus's honor. It is the town where Jesus readied himself for his triumphant entry to Jerusalem on Palm Sunday before his crucifixion (see Mark 11:1 and Luke 19:29). Here, Jesus cursed the fig tree (see Mark 11:11–13). Luke 24 tells us Bethany is the place where Jesus said his final words to the disciples before ascending into heaven after the resurrection.

This was the hometown of Mary, Martha, and Lazarus. We do not know whether their parents were alive, but there's a strong case to be made that they were deceased, since they are not mentioned in the gospel narrative.

The fact that Martha welcomed Jesus into the home indicates she was the mistress of the place. The word for welcomed here is *hupodechomai*, which means "to welcome and receive into one's home."[1] It's not obligatory, but joyfully making whoever walked into that home feel loved and known. The prefix of the word, *hupo*, means "under," connoting that Martha took Jesus under her wing, or under her care. While we often scold Martha in our minds for her busyness, this word reminds us that her hospitality was welcoming and joyful. Also, let's put ourselves in her shoes for a moment: How you would feel if thirteen hungry, thirsty men suddenly showed up on your doorstep. Would you have a welcoming attitude? Would you be stressed? Even though feeding them would be economically difficult and preparing that much food at once might be tiresome, Martha nevertheless practiced joyful hospitality when she invited them in.

Martha means "mistress," which indicates she was most likely the oldest of the three siblings, particularly since she opened the door to Jesus and his disciples. This biblical account of their meal likely depicts the beginning of what would become a strong friendship between Jesus and the siblings. After all, when Mary and Martha sent word to Jesus about Lazarus, they wrote, "Lord, your dear friend is very sick" (John 11:3b).

There's a strong indication that the family was well off, with a house large enough to host so many travelers. Some have speculated that Martha was one of the women who financially supported Jesus's ministry. If that is true, Mary's lavish display as she anointed Jesus's feet with costly perfume gives us further hints at the economic viability of the family.

In the story for which Martha is most famous, Mary is highlighted as a passionate student of Christ. But consider this as well: It is Martha who interrupts the Teacher and has a back-and-forth conversation with him, and she is the first person from the family that Jesus addresses before he raises Lazarus from the dead. They have a profound theological conversation, and Martha's words are full of faith and depth.

The Greek word used for Martha's serving may sound familiar to you: *diakonia*. It's where we get the word *deacon*, meaning "one who serves." It can also mean "ministry." Martha put feet to her faith, but there were moments when her service turned sour and she complained about the unfair division of household labor. (Early in our marriage, my husband and I often fought about this very thing. It's stressful when one person pulls more of the load than another.) Dr. Ray Pritchard of Keep Believing Ministries extrapolates her frustration when he writes,

> Martha was "cumbered," an old word related to our modern word "encumbered." To be cumbered was to be heavily burdened, as if you were wearing a concrete straitjacket. The Greek words is *perispao*, which means a mind pulled in a thousand directions . . . the word "worried" has the idea of a mind in pieces. And the word "upset" means to cause trouble.[2]

Martha was carrying the burden of serving a lot of people. She was understandably perturbed.

Jesus's rebuke to her was not that serving others is wrong. On the contrary, he also said these powerful words: "For even the Son of Man did not come to be served, but to serve, and to give his life as a ransom for many" (Mark 10:45). The Greek word "serve" there is *diakonethenai*, of which *diakonia* is a root. Martha wasn't wrong to serve. Her problem in that moment was that the act of service itself was more important to her than the one she was serving.

Just typing those words makes me pause. How many times have I gotten burned out and started "serving" Jesus with a bad attitude? Service starts with relationship, but Martha reversed the equation. She started with service, *then* approached Jesus. As Christ followers, we must first choose Jesus, sit at his feet as disciples, soak up all his beauty and wisdom, then let that overflow into service. Our service doesn't prove our discipleship; our discipleship indicates how much time we've spent with our Rabbi.

How This Applies to Hurried You

What can we learn from Martha as we battle our own sense of hurry as we attend to the details of life?

Busyness can help us find our one thing.

Jesus helped Martha in a highly teachable moment. When she was stressing and obsessing, he gently stopped her and helped her discern what was happening. He reminded her that doing things for him is less important than getting to know him. As I've been writing this book, I am also writing another one and preparing to be out of the office for several weeks. I've also had to record sixty-one podcasts before I leave. I have been on the brink of tears several times.

Why? Because the tasks were overwhelming. When we are feeling overwhelmed, we can either succumb to it or stop and realize that is not what God is calling us to. I must take a break. I must reconnect with Jesus. He is far more important than my tasks.

People who feel overlooked can tend to be workaholics. Frenetic activity with achievement is one thing you can control to get noticed and seen. We see a bit of this in Martha's interaction with Jesus. She wanted to be seen for what she was *doing*, yet Mary was commended simply for *being*. The more settled we are in our value, the more we realize that Jesus loves us as we are, the less we need to seek adulation from others through our work. Overworking can be a symptom of an overlooked heart trying desperately to be seen. Our God, El Roi, is the God who sees us. And he deserves our full attention.

It is a privilege to practice hospitality.

Before the death, resurrection, and ascension of Christ, Martha was practicing the ancient art of hospitality. Welcoming others into her home was an act of love. Many Bible passages remind us of hospitality's importance.

> "When you put on a luncheon or a banquet," [Jesus] said, "don't invite your friends, brothers, relatives, and rich neighbors. For they will invite you back, and that will be your only reward. Instead, invite the poor, the crippled, the lame, and the blind. Then at the resurrection of the righteous, God will reward you for inviting those who could not repay you." (Luke 14:12–14)

It's possible that Jesus and his disciples could not repay Martha for the food she gave them. They were itinerant and hungry. Her hospitality enabled them to do the work of the ministry. This is no small thing!

Paul reminds us that "when God's people are in need, be ready to help them. Always be eager to practice hospitality" (Romans 12:13). Peter encourages us to "Cheerfully share your home with those who need a meal or a place to stay" (1 Peter 4:9). And the author of Hebrews brings it to an interesting level: "Don't forget to show hospitality to strangers, for some who have done this have entertained angels without realizing it!" (Hebrews 13:2). Martha didn't entertain angels—she entertained the Messiah himself!

We must not dismiss the importance of making others feel important by welcoming them into our lives and giving them respite. This is where being overlooked becomes our superpower. We can use that pain as a reminder of how *not* to treat people. Because we know the sting of it, we can joyfully offer others what we have not received. There is a certain joy that comes from that.

Having a theology of suffering will serve us well.

Martha had a profound theological conversation with Jesus centered around grief. She was honest with him when she said, "Lord, if only you had been here, my brother would not have died" (John 11:21). No doubt those words were tinged with accusation and sadness. Jesus could have healed Lazarus but did not. When we experience the death of a loved one, it is not wrong to be honest with God, to let him know you don't understand his ways or why he didn't heal that person. Naming your pain is part of the grieving process.

But she didn't stop there. Martha expressed her faith in a life beyond the grave when she said, "But even now I know that God will give you whatever you ask" (verse 22). When Jesus tells her that Lazarus would rise again, she shifted into theological mode, reaffirming the idea that all will be resurrected on the last day. This statement (even in her grief) gave Jesus an opening to declare something profound.

He told her that he is the resurrection and the life. "Anyone who believes in me will live, even after dying. Everyone who lives in me and believes in me will never ever die" (verses 25–26). He then asked, "Do you believe this, Martha?"

Before we look at her answer, let's pause a moment. Martha's conversation with Jesus gives him the space to declare the Gospel to her. Jesus tells her that he is supreme even over death (foreshadowing his death, then resurrection). These are the kinds of things Jesus told his disciples to prepare them for what was to come! He was entrusting Kingdom words to her—a woman.

It also was a declaration of help for those who suffer. One day all will be made well. We who love Jesus will not remain in the grave but live eternally. When I was struggling profoundly with my own childhood trauma (including parents' divorces, an unsafe home, neglect, sexual abuse from my father, and later, his death), I came across Randy Alcorn's writings about eternal perspective. Reorienting my mind toward That Day, when my tears will be wiped away, changed the way I looked at suffering. It reframed suffering as something that is temporary, eventually giving way to the eternal weight of glory. Jesus's words to Martha echo this idea: This is not all there is. Suffering means something. Death may have temporary victory, but life will spring eternal.

When Martha answers Jesus, she acknowledges what few of his contemporaries declared: She tells Jesus who he is. "I have always believed you are the Messiah, the Son of God, the one who has come into the world from God" (verse 27). She always believed in him. *Always*. Something must've transpired in her heart when Jesus told her he was the most important thing. She believed it, then lived it. She was teachable and reachable. And she understood the aim of

Jesus, to be the Messiah and save his people. Saying he came from God also asserts his divinity. Calling him "the Son of God" reveals his authority.

No matter how overlooked we are, we can always be a friend of Jesus.

Martha wasn't just an acquaintance of Jesus; she was his close friend, as were Mary and Lazarus. Theirs was a relationship formed over time. When Lazarus died and Jesus didn't come, it was Martha who first approached *him*. This shows the reciprocity of their relationship. She sought him! Then, they had a difficult conversation, as friends do.

Perhaps the most comforting thing we can do when we are grieving, scared, feeling lost, or experiencing the pain of being overlooked is to approach Jesus honestly. He reminded his disciples of the importance of their friendship with him when he said, "I no longer call you slaves, because a master doesn't confide in his slaves. Now you are my friends, since I have told you everything the Father told me" (John 15:15).

When we feel friendless, remember we have been befriended by the One who died for us. Oswald Chambers wrote,

> The most important aspect of Christianity is not the work we do, but the relationship we maintain (with God) and the surrounding influence and qualities produced by that relationship. That is all God asks us to give our attention to, and it is the one thing that is continually under attack.[3]

We can live as if the words of God have power. Overlooked people often feel that no one talks to them. But God speaks to all of us, particularly through his Word. Think about how Martha's life was transformed by God's words to her! She moved from frenetic activity to resting in her adoration of Jesus. She deepened her faith in him through the conversations they had. And Jesus's words to dead-then-alive Lazarus certainly had resurrection power in them! She witnessed the transforming power of those words, and her life was forever altered. We must remember what Peter told Jesus when he asked whether the disciples would abandon him. "Lord, to whom would we go? You have the words that give eternal life" (John 6:68). Martha reminds us of why we should continually seek after Jesus. He is the source of our life.

We might tend to think that hurried Martha lived in a state of permanent rebuke, but her entire story shows us that she grew throughout her relationship with Jesus. She demonstrated that she had moved from hurried hostess to astute theologian. She got to watch a miracle take place before her very eyes. She is proof that even when we feel hurried, there is profound beauty in the simple, daily acts of walking out our faith as we seek after Jesus.

Truths about Unhurried You

- Hospitality is simply making people feel loved and noticed. When you feel overlooked, you can use that feeling to treat others differently.
- Women can and should study theology.
- The more we immerse ourselves in the words of God, the more we grow.

- One mistake does not define you. What Jesus continues to do through you matters.
- Jesus can do the miraculous on your behalf.

Questions for Discussion

1. How did your understanding of Martha change after reading this chapter? How did it remain the same?
2. Who, in your life, best represents hospitality to you? (Remember, hospitality is not about making food or what kind of home you have; it's about making people feel at home and welcome.)
3. What is significant about Martha's conversation with Jesus? How does he treat her when she talks with him before Lazarus's resurrection?
4. When have you been worried and bothered about a lot of things in your life? How does the example of Martha's sister Mary sitting at Jesus's feet help reframe your stress?
5. What do you think it must've been like to hug a brother who had been dead for several days?

CHAPTER NINE

Lois and Eunice, the Older Ones

Lystra bustled as the day morphed from cool and overcast to burnt-off clouds and an unrelenting sun. Lois walked the familiar route to the agora, needing to gather food for her family once again. Every day people needed food, and every day, she provided it. She walked past the pagan altars honoring Greek gods and goddesses. She closed her eyes when the shadow of Zeus's statue fell over her. Was she superstitious? No. Her Jewish allegiance to Yahweh would not allow her to worship a pantheon of gods. There was only one true God, and knowing that made the other ones ridiculous, even odious to her.

As long as Lois could remember, she had loved the scrolls of parchment that held God's words. She had studied them diligently, then passed on her fervor for God's ways to her daughter, Eunice. When chastised for her dedication to all things Torah, she quietly prayed that God would help her be a faithful Jew, one who loved Yahweh with all her heart, soul, mind, and strength. And that she'd apply the Levitical law as well—to love her neighbor as she loved herself. The *Shema*, the all-encompassing recitation of how she was to love God, infused her life, but oddly, left her wondering if there was more.

Lois thanked God for the day, for the privilege of serving her family and encouraging Eunice and now her grandson, Timothy, to be faithful to Jesus Christ and his ways. Their faith was a rare gem in a pagan land, she knew. To be Jewish after the diaspora was one problem, but then to follow a sect called The Way? Lois's friends worried about her wellbeing. Had she gone mad? Would she be persecuted?

When the Apostle Paul first visited their city, she was a Jew who had zealously searched the Scripture to fact-check everything he had said. She found herself drawn to the apostle that day—the day that changed everything for her. She learned that Paul, too, had been a zealous Jew, poring through their sacred writings and practicing righteousness even to the point of putting Christians to death. He had persecuted that which he now championed. He understood the Jewish heritage, but there was something otherworldly about him—a peace she had not seen in her fellow Jews. An internal joy that enticed her to want to know more about this Jesus of whom he spoke so eloquently.

As she neared the market and Lois reminded herself of what she needed to purchase for the gathering that night, she smiled. At this very spot, Paul and his companion Barnabas had prayed for a crippled man. Lois remembered holding her breath as she had watched. *Would their God grant such a request? And who was this Jesus to whom Paul so affectionately referred?* Every time she heard the name, her heart leapt in her chest.

She could remember every detail of that holy moment: the temperature of the day (cool), the stillness of the birds that normally chattered, the shift in the air when Paul and Barnabas noticed the beggar. Lois was familiar with the crippled man, but never knew his name. He was more fixture than person; he begged on that corner so much that he blended into the scenery. Lois chastised herself as she recalled the scene. She should have seen him as a man made in God's beautiful image—he was vulnerable, and wasn't God continually telling the Jewish people to take care of the marginalized in their path? Why hadn't she stopped to ask about him? But perhaps that's why Paul had come—to teach them all how to walk differently. To model what it meant to live a new way.

Lois stood a moment longer, remembering the scene. A crowd had gathered around Paul to hear his teaching about Jesus Christ—a Jew who claimed to be the Son of God, who died for the sins of the world once and for all, then conquered death by rising from the grave. He had told his disciples he was the way, the truth, and the life, that if anyone wanted to know the Father of all, they had to pass through him. The crippled man seemed to pay careful attention to Paul, who then nodded the man's way.

Paul had looked at Lois as if he knew her. "Who is this man?" he asked.

In that moment, she had felt seen. Noticed. Dignified.

She took a deep breath, trying to calm her heart that now beat wildly. She explained that she didn't know the man personally, but that he had been crippled since birth.

Paul made no explanation, gave no sermon. He simply shouted, "Stand up!" And the man had leapt to his feet and immediately walked. It had been Jesus who healed the man through Paul—that Lois now knew.

Shock filled her. Awe, too. *What kind of power is this? What kind of authority?* In that hesitant second between unbelief and belief, she had met the Jesus Christ whom Paul preached and demonstrated. Her life would be forever ruined for the mundane.

The crowd around the man had erupted in chaos. They thought Paul and Barnabas must be gods, that Barnabas had to have been Zeus, and that Paul was Hermes since he spoke so much. In a flurry, the crowd brought bulls and ceremonial wreaths of blooming flowers to the gates of Lystra, readying themselves to sacrifice them to their new "gods." The people did not understand that Jesus Christ, the One Paul said had died and risen on their behalf, had healed this man, nor did they grasp that their so-called gods were impotent. She briefly thought of her Greek husband, who had passed away. *Would he have sided with the crowds as well?*

The frenzy seemed to startle Paul and Barnabas. Paul spoke to the growing crowd. "Friends," he said, "why are you doing this? We are merely human beings—just like you! We have come to bring you the Good News that you should turn from these worthless things and turn to the living God, who made heaven and earth, the sea, and everything in them." Lois remembered him saying that God had allowed people like them to do whatever they wanted, but he still left them with witnesses about his nature—the sky, the stars, the sea, rain, and crops. She had missed the signs that pointed to him too. In the busyness of trying to eke out a living, she had forgotten to look up and praise God for his mighty creation.

These heavenly words did not matter to the people, she knew. When your worldview attributes everything to the actions or inaction of fickle gods, how can you easily change it in an instant? One God replacing many was blasphemy to them. A God who sacrificed his Son for the sake of humanity? No god in the pantheon would do such a ridiculous thing.

Then the Jewish rebels from Antioch and Iconium had stirred up the crowd, nearly igniting a riot. Lois had been ashamed that her countrymen could not see what she now did. Jesus Christ was the Son of God! But the crowd felt that to be blasphemy. A few weeks ago, she would have as well. But now? God had taken hold of her heart supernaturally, as miraculously as the man whose feet became un-lame.

In short order, the crowd changed from wanting to crown Paul and Barnabas as gods to stoning them and dragging them out of town. When they dispersed, Lois searched beyond the gates of Lystra and found the men—bleeding and breathing heavily, but blessedly alive. Paul was muttering about a third heaven, the beauty of Jesus, and the privilege of suffering for the Body of Christ. She tended to his and Barnabas's wounds before they left the next day for Derbe. She had begged them to stay, but they'd been compelled by God to leave.

Shaking herself of the reverie, Lois continued her journey to the market, grateful for life and the testimony of Paul. His bravery had ignited something in her that she did not know she had—her own ability to boldly share about Jesus Christ no matter what happened to her. She would declare it boldly to her family and anyone else who would listen. She had hung on to Paul's words during his most recent brief visit, and she learned the importance of making disciples of the people closest to her.

That's why she poured her life into Eunice and young Timothy, who welcomed her tutelage. They needed to know that God saw them and would take care of them. They were no longer widowed or orphaned; they were wanted and had been adopted into a new family.

Paul's letter to their small body of believers quickened Lois's resolve to excel in teaching rightly about Jesus Christ and what it meant to follow him. Bad teaching had already infiltrated their ranks, so she spent more time studying the Torah and every jot and tittle of Paul's letters. She recalled as many stories of Jesus as she could remember—told by Paul and other travelers who followed The Way. She did not want to be bewitched by errant teaching. She wanted to be free to follow heartily after Jesus Christ, to honor him in everything she did. Sometimes she was confused by her Jewish brothers and sisters who insisted on having her keep parts of their ancient law, but Paul reminded them all that it was for freedom that Christ had come, and that they should not subject themselves to other religious practices. Otherwise, the beautiful cross meant nothing. If she had to do other things (other than exercising her faith in Jesus) to be saved, then the Gospel was not the Gospel. Christ and his sacrifice on her behalf alone could redeem a person. Nothing more. Nothing less.

Paul wrote of the importance of bearing burdens without complaint—something Lois took quite seriously, particularly on market day. She exchanged her usual pleasantries with her favorite merchants, purchased fresh vegetables and berries, found a nice cut of lamb, and hurried home.

"Hello, my dear Eunice," she trilled as she entered the house. "I have everything you asked for."

Eunice greeted her with a kiss, one on each cheek. They busied themselves over the meal, preparing for the evening meeting with the rest of the *ecclesia*. These love feasts were how they celebrated Jesus—his life, death, and resurrection. Before celebrating the sacrament of the Lord's supper that he taught his disciples to do on his last night on earth, they ate a full meal together. Theirs was a gathering of people from all backgrounds, bound together by faith, friendship, and food.

"I wish we could hear from Timothy," Lois said as she stuffed the lamb with herbs and olive oil.

Eunice wiped away a tear. "I miss him."

"We both do." Lois put an arm around her daughter. They had sent Timothy, whose name aptly meant "one who honors God," with Paul to be his companion and disciple. Paul had asked Timothy to accompany him on his second visit to Lystra—something that thrilled yet scared Lois. *What would happen to him?* Paul's journeys were known to be fraught with danger. Would Timothy suffer similar persecutions? Her grandson had a special gift, she knew. There had been prophecies, the laying on of hands, and words of encouragement to him within their congregation. Paul had noticed right away that Timothy had a fire in his eyes and a strength of spirit that belied his age.

"But we prepared him well," Lois concluded.

"He has become like a son to Paul," Eunice said. "That alone is enough for me." She tossed vegetables in olive oil and salt, readying them for roasting.

Lois took the vegetables from her and placed them on their outdoor brazier. The smell of roasted leeks made her smile, as it always did. "There is one thing I wonder about." She sat on the ledge surrounding their small courtyard.

"What is that?" Eunice asked, sitting next to her.

"Well, we have learned from Paul that the men in our congregation should not get circumcised. If our men do that, then it means that Christ died needlessly." Lois swatted away a fly.

Eunice coughed. "Yes, you are correct. But it's hard to think that way since you and I both have steeped ourselves in the Torah. Circumcision is a part of our heritage, a sign of God's covenant with Abraham."

"And we, together, have saturated our dear Timothy with those powerful words—of covenants, promises, freedom, exile, and return from exile." Eunice stood and shifted the roasting vegetables, then adjusted the spit. "So what is it that is bothering you, dear Mother?"

"Paul asked Timothy to be circumcised. Why would he do that? Is he being inconsistent?"

Eunice smiled. "It is confusing, but I have corresponded with Timothy about this. I am sorry I forgot to show you." She went into the house, then returned with a scroll. "Here it is." She scanned the document. "Paul does believe Gentiles should not be circumcised, but because Timothy is half Jewish, Paul felt it important not to put up a stumbling block to the Gospel when they encountered fellow Jews."

She read further, then looked up. "In our case here in Lystra, the Judaizers wanted to force all Gentiles to be circumcised, which would pervert the Gospel, but with our Timothy, Paul was thinking primarily of those Jews who had yet to believe. Timothy writes . . ."

She dropped her eyes to read directly from the text. "Paul wrote this to the church in Corinth, 'Though I am free and belong to no one, I have made myself a slave to everyone, to win as many as possible. To the Jews I became like a Jew, to win the Jews. To those under the law I became like one under the law (though I myself am not under the law), so as to win those under the law.'"

"So, he is saying that Paul deals differently with those in the church than those without?" Lois stood up and tested the lamb. It would take at least another hour to fully cook. Thankfully, their congregation wouldn't arrive for another two.

Eunice nodded. "Yes, I think that is the point. Paul wrote, 'To the weak I became weak, to win the weak. I have become all things to all people so that by all possible means I might save some. I do this all for the sake of the Gospel, that I may share in its blessings.'"

She rolled the scroll back up. "Maybe we should read this letter to the church tonight. I think it might encourage our friends."

Lois gathered blankets from beneath a bench and began spreading them out to prepare for the gathering. "Excellent idea. Thank you for sharing that with me. I know our dear Timothy would not want any sort of stumbling block between our fellow countrymen who don't yet understand The Way." She finished placing the blankets just so, then turned to Eunice. "But I have to say, I am also very encouraged that Paul does not want our Greek brothers to be circumcised—at their age, it would be a painful endeavor."

They laughed as the sun began its gradual descent over Lystra. The meat turned slowly on the spit. The vegetables were plated. She prepared dessert. Wine was poured into vessels. In the lull between preparation and gathering, Lois prayed that Timothy would be a vessel for honor, carrying within him the very Kingdom of God.

"Please protect my grandson," she prayed out loud. "Keep him strong."

The Biblical Narrative

These two Jewish women, Lois and Eunice, were most likely part of the Jewish diaspora that sent Jewish people outside of Israel to the far reaches of the Roman empire during Roman persecution. You can find them in 2 Timothy 1 and 3. Lois's family settled in the city of Lystra, located in modern-day Turkey. The fact that both Lois and Eunice have Greek names indicates they assimilated into their culture. *Lois* means "most beautiful,"[1] and *Eunice* means "good victory."[2] They both married Greek men, which would account for Timothy's lack of circumcision. Timothy's name is also Greek and means "honoring God." Though Scripture is silent on the matter, it's possible that Timothy's Greek father had prohibited him from being circumcised. It's also interesting to note that although there are many grandmothers throughout Scripture, Lois is the only one specifically identified that way. Paul writes:

> I remember your genuine faith, for you share the faith that first filled your grandmother Lois and your mother,

> Eunice. And I know that same faith continues strong in you. (2 Timothy 1:5)

Some scholars believe that because Paul seems to be familiar with Timothy's family, he may have known or been related to them, but the Scripture is silent on that matter.

A second reference to Timothy's upbringing also fleshes out these faithful women:

> But you must remain faithful to the things you have been taught. You know they are true, for you know you can trust those who taught you. You have been taught the holy Scriptures from childhood, and they have given you the wisdom to receive the salvation that comes by trusting in Christ Jesus. All Scripture is inspired by God and is useful to teach us what is true and to make us realize what is wrong in our lives. It corrects us when we are wrong and teaches us to do what is right. God uses it to prepare and equip his people to do every good work. (2 Timothy 3:14–17)

What a profound statement about the power of God's Word!

Let's unpack Paul's meaning in these verses:

- Timothy's faith was built upon what he had already learned from the Old Testament.
- His mother and grandmother were faithful; they could be trusted. In other words, they were effective and righteous teachers of the Law.
- Not only did they impart the Scriptures, but they also taught Timothy how to be wise. It's one thing to know *about* God; it's another to act on that knowledge wisely.

- All three members of the family came to faith in Jesus Christ at some point. Most believe this happened the first time Paul visited Lystra. The second time, he commissioned Timothy and took him on his next mission.
- Both the Old and New Testaments help us know God better and discern what is true. (Note: Remember, the only Scriptures Lois and Eunice had were the Old Testament books of the Law and the Prophets, as well as the Psalms and Proverbs. The New Testament was being written in their time, mostly in the form of letters from Paul to various churches.)
- Scripture tells us when we are walking the wrong way. It is vital and necessary for the one who follows God to read it regularly and take it to heart.
- God has prepared good works for us to do (see Ephesians 2:10). Knowing his Word helps us to do them.

No doubt Lois and Eunice knew the nature of God's beautiful Word. They would've known the history of Israel, as they inherited its promises from God. As devout Jewish expatriates, they still adhered to the ancient texts that defined their position as children of God.

What's beautiful about these two is that their knowledge of the Torah was not a stumbling block to their belief in Christ. Where Paul's expertise in matters of religious law led him initially to persecute Christians, Eunice and Lois followed Jesus after hearing about Him. Perhaps they were like the Bereans of Macedonia. Luke writes about them in Acts 17:11:

> And the people of Berea were more open-minded than those in Thessalonica, and they listened eagerly to Paul's message. They searched the Scriptures day after day to see if Paul and Silas were teaching the truth.

Lois and Eunice's love for the Old Testament paved the path of faith for Timothy.

How This Applies to Older You

Paul was fond of Lois and Eunice and did not overlook them. But we often do because they're not given much mention in the New Testament. Yet their lives give us valuable lessons about how to live for Christ.

Teaching the Word of God is never a waste of time. Lois and Eunice, though in a Greek context, knew the importance of sharing the Scriptures with the next generation. Of course, Moses's words in Deuteronomy would've echoed through them because they first contain the *Shema*. "Listen, O Israel! The Lord is our God, the Lord alone. And you must love the Lord your God with all your heart, all your soul, and all your strength. And you must commit yourselves wholeheartedly to these commands that I am giving you today" (Deuteronomy 4:4–6). Moses doesn't end with the beautiful theology of loving God with everything inside us. Instead, we must teach it to the next generations. "Repeat them again and again to your children. Talk about them when you are at home and when you are on the road, when you are going to bed and when you are getting up. Tie them to your hands and wear them on your forehead as reminders. Write them on the doorposts of your house and on your gates" (Deuteronomy 6:7–9). Theirs was a faith that was caught, then taught, then exemplified.

They took seriously the mandate of the Psalmist to share about the faithfulness of God to their families. "We will not hide these truths from our children; we will tell the next generation about the glorious deeds of the Lord, about his power and his mighty wonders. For he issued his laws to Jacob; he gave his instructions to Israel. He commanded our ancestors to teach them to their children, so the next generation might know them—even the children not yet born—and they in turn will teach their own children" (Psalm 78:4–6). They understood that sharing God's exploits were their privilege, and that in doing so, they were creating a legacy.

Some of the most overlooked workers in Christendom today are those who teach children. Yet, we see in Eunice and Lois's faithfulness the emergence of Timothy, who had a profound impact on the early church. Pouring into the next generation may not be accompanied by fanfare, but it can exponentially impact the world with ripples that affect generations to come. If you are in this place, remember the words of Zechariah when he prophesied about the completion of the Temple—an endeavor that started small. "Do not despise these small beginnings, for the Lord rejoices to see the work begin" (Zechariah 4:10a).

Authenticity begats disciples.

As we look at the Greek in 2 Timothy 1:5 where Lois and Eunice are mentioned, we come across an interesting verb. The word "genuine," or in other translations, "sincere" is *anupokritos*, which literally means to *not* pretend.[3] If you look closely at the word, you can see the root of *hypocrisy* there. In other words, to have a genuine faith like Lois and Eunice is to be the opposite of a hypocrite. Paul uses the word in connection with love in Romans 12:9. "Don't just pretend to love others. Really love them. Hate what is wrong. Hold tightly to what is good." He makes the same equation in 2 Corinthians 6:6. "We prove ourselves by our purity, our understanding, our patience, our kindness, by the Holy Spirit within us, and by our sincere love." Our love, then, must be genuine.

Eunice and Lois had a real faith that translated in the way they treated Timothy. They not only knew God and his ways, but they also taught them sincerely. And the words they taught translated into their behavior. Not only did they emulate the *Shema* (loving God with everything inside them), but they also let that love inform the way they treated others.

Today we are facing a crisis in the church, where people are questioning what they experienced in church, then deconstruct their faith. One of the reasons (the issue is complex) they do that is that the actions of those proclaiming faith did not match up with their beliefs. Authenticity is a high value of the next generations, and they have an inbred ability to smell a rat when it comes to hypocrisy. To live an authentic, faith-filled life may not be glamorous, and it may not get you onto a platform or a stage, but it's this quiet pouring into others the sincere faith you have that truly makes disciples. Isn't that how Jesus did it? Constantly overlooked by those whose piety was on display, Jesus chose the obscure routes for world change. He, who is the Truth, poured that truth into disciples who later turned the world upside down for the Gospel.

In the quiet place, you are not overlooked.

Eunice and Lois did the work of discipleship for Timothy in the margins of their lives. They did not seek center stage, but they quietly learned the word of God, then taught it. God takes note of that. Even when you are overlooked by others, those small, seemingly insignificant acts are taken note of by the One who fashioned you. The Greek word for "filled" (or in other translations, dwelt) is *enoikeo* and literally means "to indwell, to take up residence." This is only a metaphor—it doesn't literally mean to be in someone's home.[4] This is the same word Paul uses in 2 Timothy 1:14 when he speaks of the indwelling Holy Spirit. The faith of Eunice and Lois was a surefire reality; it was in their bones, lived out in fidelity. It had become so much a part of their way of doing life that you could not separate them from their faith; they were so intertwined.

When we have that kind of vital "at homeness" with Christ, the sting of being overlooked fades. We are loved and noticed by the One who fashioned us. We can settle our value there. We are held when the world spins out of control.

Teaching children is vitally important.

We live in an adult world where all the flash of ministry is dedicated to those emerging into adulthood (teens) or those who are adults. But if you really want to bring impact to the world, start noticing and teaching children. I think about my own longing as a child. I only went to church once as an elementary student, to be baptized. I had the opportunity to attend one Sunday School class before the ceremony. I still remember it. I recall how I felt, how I was treated by the sweet Sunday School teacher. Because the adults in my life were *not* acting like Lois and Eunice (in any way, shape, or form), in that deprivation, I soaked up attention from an older adult. I was an overlooked kid, but had I had the chance to return to Sunday School (I begged my mom to no avail), I can only imagine the kind of life change I would've experienced.

Never, ever underestimate the importance of teaching children the things of God. The entire landscape of the kingdom of God was changed through the ministry of Timothy, thanks to these two women who valued children as much as Jesus did. "Let the children come to me. Don't stop them! For the Kingdom of God belongs to those who are like these children," Jesus said in Mark 10:14b. Teaching young minds about the Good News is one of the most beautiful ways to impact future generations. Don't lose heart. Don't let the world's dismissal of children influence you. Like Lois and Eunice, pour your authentic faith into children.

While Lois and Eunice do not take up much biblical real estate, their impact can be felt to this day. Paul's words to Timothy are canon. The church experienced growth and depth because of Timothy's missionary journeys and influence. Never underestimate the value of pouring your authentic life into others. It's a down payment you make for eternity.

Truths about Legacy-Making You

- When you authentically live out your faith, people notice.
- The Scriptures are clear: Women who pour themselves into the Word of God leave a legacy in the world.
- Our families are a beautiful mission field.
- In a world full of flashy, famous ministers, God notices people who make disciples of others in unknown and unsung corners of the Kingdom.
- Your work for the Lord is never, ever wasted.

Questions for Discussion

1. What did you know about Lois and Eunice before reading this chapter?
2. Why do you think the issue of circumcision may have been confusing for Timothy and other early believers?
3. Chances are that Eunice was a widow. How does her story help you understand God's heart for those society marginalizes?

4. Who in your life do you have the chance to influence for the Gospel? Who poured into you when you were younger?
5. What does it mean to you to disciple another person? How does the example of Lois and Eunice encourage you?

CHAPTER TEN

Junia(s), the Misnamed One

Junia made her way to Jerusalem during the feast of Pentecost. She was not accustomed to the hustle of the marketplace, but she persisted, sometimes having to elbow her way through the crowd toward the great and beautiful Temple. The sun beat hot upon her brow, and her head covering stifled her further.

A great rush of noise swirled around her like a mighty wind, stopping her in her tracks. The crowd around her began shouting joyfully, all in different languages. More people came running as the commotion intensified. Junia could identify some of the languages—Roman, Egyptian, Libyan—and all the messages were the same. "God has done mighty things! God is great! Look at all the marvelous things our God has performed!"

Someone next to her turned her way, asking, "What can this mean?"

Junia did not know.

Another person nearby sneered, "They're just drunk, that's all!"

Others murmured their agreement, but Junia was not convinced. How could drunken people so clearly articulate the greatness of God in so many languages at one time?

She thought back on her nation's history, how they'd endured so much—enslavement, then emancipation from Egypt, conquering Canaan, the era of the judges and kings, the divided kingdom, the Babylonian exile, and then the return to Israel. God had been quite silent for several hundred years, though Junia had sought him often. And now here she stood—experiencing some sort of divine interaction! Was God visiting his people afresh?

A man pushed through the crowd, found a step, then stood on it. She did not recognize him, though his garb and dialect suggested he was an everyday worker from Galilee, perhaps a fisherman.

"Listen carefully, all of you, fellow Jews and residents of Jerusalem!" he cried. "Make no mistake about this. These people are not drunk, as some of you are assuming. Nine o'clock in the morning is much too early for that. No, what you see was predicted long ago by the prophet Joel—"

Junia recognized the reference to God's promise to pour his Spirit upon all people—not just special ones, but young people, old people, rich people, and servants alike. When he did, miracles would happen. She mouthed the last part of Joel's words with the man. "—but everyone who calls on the name of the Lord will be saved."

That word, *saved*. She felt it in her gut. She knew she needed to be rescued from her own propensity to do wrong. All her life she had searched the holy words of the Law and Prophets. What could all this mean?

The man spoke of Jesus of Nazareth. She had heard rumors of him healing people, delivering the demonized, and feeding thousands of people with only five loaves of bread and two small fish.

He had been known as a good teacher before the Romans had crucified him recently, but she had not really given him much thought. She had her own experiences with men who purported to be revolutionary, only to have their missions die when they fell into the grave.

The man on the step interrupted her thoughts as he continued, "But God released him from the horrors of death and raised him back to life, for death could not keep him in its grip." He went on to quote King David, about the way of life. These words caught Junia's attention. How many times had she begged the Lord to show her the pathway to life?

The man raised his hands to the heavens and pointed out that King David had died and not risen again, like all their forefathers. But Jesus? "God raised Jesus from the dead, and we are all witnesses of this." He pointed to the growing group of people to Junia's left. "Now he is exalted to the place of highest honor in heaven, at God's right hand."

The man's voice carried over the entire marketplace. Where it had been filled with the voices of merchants and shoppers just a few minutes earlier, now everyone stood silent, soaking in his words. "So let everyone in Israel know for certain that God has made this Jesus, whom you crucified, to be both Lord and Messiah!"

She felt a piercing sensation in her heart. *This Jesus? The one who was crucified, then resurrected?* She wanted to know him—but how?

The person next to her shouted, "Brother, what should we do?"

The man spoke of turning away from sins, then turning toward God. Junia felt the wooing of the Father in that moment. In her mind, she told God how sorry she was for the many sins she had committed, for which no animal sacrifice could completely atone. At the mention of the Holy Spirit, Junia fell to her knees, overwhelmed by the presence of the God she had pursued all her life. In this holy moment, it was as if she were meeting him for the first time.

Relief flooded through her. Tears erupted from the depth of her broken heart. Each sob cleansed her afresh. She could not help but speak of God's mighty deeds of old while anticipating that he would do even more in her time. The man on the step, whom she later learned was named Peter, spoke of baptism as a public declaration of what had just happened in her heart—dying to sin and rising to a brand-new life.

The crowd moved toward the ancient *mikvahs* nearby, the baths meant to cleanse Jews who had been ceremonially unclean upon their return to society. One by one, Peter and his companions dipped people into the water as a symbol of death, then pulled them back out as a sign of resurrection.

When Junia swooshed into the cool, clear water, she thought of her fellow Jews who had been rescued from oppression, slavery, and death through the Red Sea. And as she gasped and coughed her way back into the sunlight, Junia knew her life would never be the same. Like her people after the Exodus, she was no longer enslaved, but blessedly free.

Junia struggled against her shackles, waiting for her husband, Andronicus, to join her in the hymn she was singing. She relished his baritone from the other corner of their dank cell; suffering for Jesus had been worth every sacrifice. Their zeal for the things of God had been muted before their conversion to The Way—proper even—but when she truly met Jesus Christ, he set her life ablaze. That blaze was what had attracted the attention of Andronicus, another freed slave like herself. Once married, the church in Jerusalem sent them to various parts of the Roman Empire to proclaim God's powerful plan of salvation for the whole world.

Through the scurrying of rats and the rumbling of her stomach, Junia reminded herself that this life mattered not. So she sang even louder. Blood ran from a wound on her head, but she could not wipe it free.

"How is my beautiful bride?" Andronicus wheezed. His cough had deepened, as had his voice.

"I am well," she said. It wasn't the whole truth, but it was true enough.

They both knew their conditions were among the worst the Roman Empire had to offer its prisoners. At first, Junia had feared they would be separated, but the Roman penal system observed no such dichotomy. She thanked the good Lord that they were together. She had heard rumors of guards taking advantage of female prisoners; at least with Andronicus, she was safe from that. The sores on her backside and legs had grown larger, and if she shut her eyes in sleep, the rats chewed at them until she woke to their gnawing and yelled them away.

Into this fellowship of the darkness, a light pierced.

Without warning, the barred door of their cell creaked open, and a shell of a man was shoved into it. Junia screamed in alarm. But as soon as the Roman guard had left, the man, still unchained, looked at her and said quietly, "I am Paul, the apostle."

She had heard of this man! Formerly, he had been known as Saul—a very learned man who had been so zealous for the legalistic Jewish faith that he had hunted Christians like her—chased them down across Israel to murder them. But that had changed one day when he was on his way to Damascus—she'd heard that a light had blinded him, and Jesus himself had spoken to him from it, telling him to stop persecuting his people. The encounter had so radically changed Saul that three days later, when God miraculously healed him of his blindness, he had become a follower of The Way himself. Now he traveled all throughout Asia Minor spreading the news of Jesus and teaching other believers his ways. And he had the scars to prove that others found the message just as offensive as he once had. This man had been beaten and even stoned for the sake of the Gospel he now loudly proclaimed.

And now he was here, in their cell.

Thus began a short stint of fellowship that would enflame Junia for the rest of her days. She, Andronicus, and Paul spent several days speaking about Jesus's life, death, and resurrection, Paul's encounter with him on the road to Damascus, and their own testimonies of faith. Paul intertwined his knowledge of the Torah with a new apologetic for the church of Jesus Christ. He encouraged them both to stay faithful to his calling to welcome persecution as normal and to rely wholly on the Holy Spirit's guidance, conviction, and encouragement.

He told them stories of being shipwrecked in blustery seas and the beatings and ostracism he'd endured from his fellow Jews. Together, they sang hymns of praise and recited psalms written by King David. They told him of their exploits sharing the Good News with Jews and Gentiles alike and listened as Paul told them of his passion to become all things to all people so that he might welcome many into the beautiful Kingdom of God. Though Paul only remained with them a few days before being transferred to a different prison, their time together proved to be a divine gift.

"I will always remember you, Junia," Paul told her before he was taken away.

"And I, you," she choked out, wondering if she would see him again this side of eternity.

"Continue your work without wavering." Paul stood, then

paced as if he knew the guards were on their way. "Remember, he who began a good work in you will complete it. Don't be afraid. Stay strong. Do the work of an evangelist."

"And you, Andronicus, my friend," Paul said. "Stay faithful. Continue to teach others about Jesus Christ."

Andronicus thanked him, then said a prayer that wafted behind Paul as he was taken away. He turned toward Junia. "Do you think we'll ever see him again?"

She shook her head. "I don't know. I hope so."

The couple did not encounter Paul later as they made their way toward Rome, but his fingerprints were everywhere. It was as if the Lord had prepared a way for them through their friend's pioneering efforts. Every time they entered a city, they found Paul had already been there, sharing the Good News, mostly with Gentiles. It made their work joyful and light, as if they were two among many faithful workers. This was the beauty of the church, Junia knew. Some people tilled the soil; others planted little seeds, small as a mustard. Some watered those tiny seeds. Some provided sunshine, and still others tended the young plants by getting rid of the weeds that popped up as they took root and grew. But through their adventures in sharing the Good News, God alone brought the harvest.

Junia and Andronicus found a home with fellow believers in Rome named Priscilla and Aquila. Together, they continued the Apostle Paul's work in establishing a thriving community of believers in the middle of the Great Satan, the Roman Empire—the very empire that had enslaved her and her husband alike in years gone by. "We are free," Andronicus continued to remind her. And she would reply with a smile.

One day, while they were hard at work at their tent-sewing business, a knock sounded at the outer door. Junia looked at Priscilla, who nodded. They had to be careful who they let in, as they were surrounded by spies. Everyone in their community had been imprisoned at least once and knew the risks of living in the heart of Rome. Junia settled her nerves, then answered the door. In front of her stood a woman, travel weary and unkempt.

"May I help you?" Junia asked.

"I am Phoebe," the woman said. "And I bear a letter from Paul."

Junia flung open the door, welcoming the woman into their midst. The three women found instant friendship as they praised God for victories and mourned some losses. That evening, Phoebe read the letter aloud to their small community.

Junia breathlessly soaked in Paul's words—the depth of theology, the beauty of the Gospel. The truths he had shared with her and Andronicus were even better reasoned, fully realized now—as if his trials had caused the bones of his words to take on flesh and dance. As Phoebe neared the end of the scroll, she read, "Give my greetings to Priscilla and Aquila, my coworkers in the ministry of Christ Jesus. In fact, they once risked their lives for me. I am thankful to them, and so are all the Gentile churches. Also give my greetings to the church that meets in their home." A hearty cheer erupted from the group, and Junia noticed Priscilla blushing. High praise from the Apostle Paul, to be sure.

"Greet my dear friend Epenetus. He was the first person from the province of Asia to become a follower of Christ." Phoebe paused. "Is he here?"

"No, we sent him to a nearby province to share the Gospel," Aquila said.

Phoebe read about Mary, and then stopped. She looked at Junia, who reached for Andronicus's hand and smiled. "Greet Andronicus and Junia, my fellow Jews, who were in prison with me. They are highly respected among the apostles and became followers of Christ before I did."

Phoebe continued reading, but Junia's mind was now back in the impossibly dank prison cell and the conversations they'd shared with Paul that had been so sweet. *The problem with life is that you live it*, she thought, *but you never really know the significance of a moment until you recount it later*. She looked at the sky and thanked God for considering her faithful and putting her into service. She would relish this time with Phoebe, but later she would kneel alongside Andronicus, asking the Lord of the Harvest to send workers (them!) back into the Roman world. The harvest was plentiful, after all, but the workers were few.

The Biblical Narrative

You may not have heard of Junia from Romans 16. For hundreds of years, translators changed her name from Junia to Junias to pass her off as a male; they could not conceive of an apostle being a woman (we'll discuss this in more detail in a moment).[1] But modern scholars nearly unanimously agree that Junia was female, and Paul's use of the word "apostle" in referencing her was no mistake. As mentioned above, Romans 16:7 says,

> Greet Andronicus and Junia, my fellow Jews, who were in prison with me. They are highly respected among the apostles and became followers of Christ before I did.

When I wrote the fictional narrative for Junia, I thought it would be interesting to have her meet Christ on the Day of Pentecost. This works within the timeline, as Paul mentioned she knew Christ before he did. I also had her marry Andronicus, though other scholars believe he could have been her brother or coworker. (We won't know which it was on this side of heaven because the Scripture is silent about their relationship.) Some people have speculated that both Junia and Andronicus were freed slaves, so I incorporated that into the narrative.[2] That they both preached the Gospel and were imprisoned for their faith (along with Paul), is not in question.

Paul often closed his letters with instructions to greet people "with a holy kiss"; this is personal, like a hug would be today. Paul has great affection for Junia and Andronicus. When he says they are "highly respected," he uses the Greek word *episemos*. This means "to have a mark upon," and it is "used literally to describe money that had been stamped or coined (with a mark)."[3] Junius and Andronicus had impact.

The Greek word for "apostles" should look familiar: *Apostolos*. And therein lies the controversy.

Some scholars have reasoned that a woman could not be an apostle, so they masculinized her name to "Junias." The problem with that is

> that the masculine name "Junias" never occurs in any ancient documents apart from a reference attributed to Epiphanius, and he also refers to Prisca as a man. The feminine name "Junia" is common enough in ancient inscriptions, and, apart from Epiphanius, church fathers such as Chrysostom, Origen, and Jerome all took Junia to be a woman.[4]

The fact that Junia is mentioned as part of the company of the apostles puts her in a pantheon of people such as Jesus's twelve disciples, Paul, Barnabas, Timothy, Silas, Apollos, and Epaphroditus.

The word simply means "someone who is sent on a mission." As we look at the dawn of the church, we see both men and women who were sent from their hometowns to spread the Gospel. Junia's work on behalf of the Lord Jesus landed her in prison, so she certainly fulfilled her role as a sent one. Whether you interpret her as an actual apostle or as an evangelistic missionary sent to further the Gospel, the truth remains—she boldly walked in her calling.

What's interesting about Junia is that she was not overlooked by her friend the Apostle Paul, but she was by historians. For those of us who deeply desire to leave a profound legacy, this hits close to home. We want to make a difference in our sphere of influence, and we want to know that our words and our lives have made an impact for eternity. The good news is that God holds all our stories in his hands, and he has a beautiful plan that will all make sense in eternity.

Friend, your calling is not in vain. Your work will not be obliterated. God uses all our obedience for his glory and for the betterment of his Kingdom.

How This Applies to Misnamed You

What can we learn from Junia?

Do it anyway.

Junia didn't wait for permission to serve God. She simply listened to the guidance of the Spirit within her and obeyed, come what may. And that "come what may" meant that she suffered imprisonment. Even so, God gave her a surprising gift—the Apostle Paul to talk to during her imprisonment. Imagine the rich theological conversations they must have had. I like to imagine that meeting Paul inspired Junia to continue the work, even if it meant further imprisonment and persecution. Perhaps she felt, as Paul wrote, "For to me, to live is Christ and to die is gain" (Philippians 1:21). Whether you're overlooked, misunderstood, maligned, or misnamed, others' disqualification of you cannot negate God's calling on your life. Do what he calls you to do anyway.

Value community.

If you feel overlooked by other Christians, you may tend to isolate from them because being overlooked causes a deep wound. Why go back to the people who have snubbed you? I wouldn't advise returning to unsafe people; Proverbs is full of relational advice about who to connect with, who to avoid, and how we are to guard our heart. But, if you want to grow as a person and experience healing from the wound of being overlooked, you need to find good, strong, healthy community. To do ministry in isolation is a prescription for burnout.

It's also interesting to note that Romans 16 tells us ministry work was not segregated; men and women didn't minister in different spheres, such as men doing all the preaching and women doing all the children's ministry. Instead, we see both genders working together for the common good.

Have conversations.

Imagine what it must've been like to be chained next to the Apostle Paul! Paul's greeting to Junia and Andronicus in Romans 16 reflects genuine friendship. While being confined with one another, they would have had ample opportunity to talk about the Kingdom of God and the Great Commission. No doubt those conversations encouraged all three of them to remain faithful.

Jesus tells us to do two things: to love God fiercely and to love others with passion. He equates the two. What that means is this:

How we love others demonstrates how we love Jesus. To love others is to spend time with them, asking questions, listening to their stories. It's to bear their burdens, share our own, encourage each other on to victory over our obstacles, to weep and laugh with them. But so often in our overburdened world, the first things we let slide are our relationships—which are fueled by conversation. (Texting is not a conversation.) Face-to-face interaction is vitally important if we want to live robust lives in community with others.

To love God is to listen to God and do what he says. Junia did that.

To love others is to listen to them and hear what they have to say. Junia did that.

Even if you feel overlooked by others, the truth remains: You are not overlooked by our God. And he will empower you to be a relational light in our texting-crazy, impersonal, online world. I love what Paul tells the Thessalonican church about his connection to them: "We loved you so much that we shared with you not only God's Good News but our own lives, too" (1 Thessalonians 2:8).

While Junia may not be well known to today's believers, she was known by Paul. She worked diligently to share the Gospel with a dying world, and she was commended for doing so. How beautiful to know that the Lord also takes note of us when we are quietly doing the work of his Kingdom!

Truths about Named You

- Even if others misrepresent you, God sees your work and will reward you.
- All of us are missionaries, sent out into the world to declare the Gospel.

- The work of the Kingdom will be more joyful when done alongside fellow believers.

Questions for Discussion

1. Were you familiar with Junia before reading this chapter? What did you learn after reading it? What questions do you still have?
2. What kind of faith did Junia have that would have enabled her to suffer being incarcerated for it? How does that encourage you?
3. What does Junia's life teach you about fidelity to Jesus?
4. Recall a time when you had the privilege of working with a team of people to disciple others and/or share the Gospel. How did the team aspect of the work help you? How was it difficult?
5. Who in your life exemplifies Junia's willingness to suffer for her faith? How does that person's walk with God inspire you?

Conclusion

Let's revisit the sixth chapter of Acts, where we see Paul's instructions for taking care of widows who were being overlooked by the early church. Because God's heart is always bent toward the broken, their outcry was important to address. Widows needed help; if they were overlooked, it could mean their demise. Jesus's disciples got together and appointed seven men to oversee the distribution of food in the newly minted church, ensuring that the forgotten would no longer be overlooked.

And that is our mandate too. When we are overlooked, it feels terrible. We experience the bewilderment of not being included or our needs being dismissed. This pain, thankfully, is something we can take to Jesus. But it is also a beautiful impetus to do things differently. We may be overlooked, but we need not overlook others. In fact, choosing others and noticing them becomes one of the most joyful endeavors we can undertake as we walk out our years on earth.

Why?

Because it's the opposite of the world's system. The world says only the shiny, or important, people deserve attention. The world dictates that wealth can buy admiration.

The world bestows value on the successful. The world creates impossible standards of beauty that only a small segment of the population can achieve. The world says you are what you do, so when you lose your "usefulness," you also lose your value. The world reminds us that we must clamber over others to succeed. The world praises the go-getters while dismissing the people the go-getters walked over.

The world encourages us to be our own hero and to get what we want. I believe Jesus is giving us new eyes in these last days—eyes to see those in our midst who others cannot see. To perceive the needs of those who don't even share their pain out loud. To become empathetic listeners to those even the church has forgotten.

Do you want to be more like Jesus?

Remember that he was often overlooked. Isaiah 53:2 tells us, "He had no beauty or majesty to attract us to him, nothing in his appearance that we should desire him." Though he was heralded as a king one day, he was decried as a criminal twenty-four hours later. He was betrayed by a close friend. He didn't have a flashy kingdom as he walked the earth. He didn't take what was his—instead, he emptied himself for our sake. He poured himself out. He gave. The Overlooked One did not overlook us. Instead, he died for us.

Let's start a revolution of truly seeing those whom society marginalizes. Let's do as the apostles did in Acts 6 and take care of the overlooked.

And may we remember the lessons these overlooked women from Scripture have taught us:

- From Tamar of Judah—to trust that God will work on our behalf.
- From Miriam—to actively help those in need.
- From Zelophehad's daughters—to speak up when we're overlooked.
- From Deborah—to boldly face opposition.
- From Abigail—to thrive even through a difficult relationship.
- From Jehosheba—to do what is right, no matter the cost.
- From Anna—to finish well.
- From Martha—to become a friend of Jesus.
- From Lois and Eunice—to pour into the next generation.
- From Junia—to be a missionary in our context, no matter the consequence.

I pray this book has empowered you to walk through healing from the pain of being overlooked. I pray it has helped you realize you are not alone in feeling that way. And I pray that you become a "noticer" of others in your everyday journey. Why? Because God has never, ever overlooked you. He is for you. He sees you. He notices you. He hears you. He loves you.

Go forth, oh noticed one!

Acknowledgments

Thank you to the team at Skyhorse Publishing who brought shape to this book. Thank you to Karla Dial, Julie Jayne, Jennifer Valk, and Kathryn Riggs for our initial brainstorming call around this book. I appreciate you, dear agent Joy Eggerichs, for your tenacity as we finalized this partnership. *Tu es tres sympa et inteligente!*

My prayer team, the Writing Prayer Circle, prays me through every manuscript. Huge thanks to Jenny, Amy, Avril, Melissa, Kathy, Tabea, Roblee, Sabrina, Susan, Misty, Rebecca C., Patti, Cheryl, Misti, Aldyth, Ally, Amy, Elaine, Dusty, Paula, Kendra, Boz, Cristin, Yanci, Paul, Brandilyn, Richard, Sue, Christy, Alice, Susie, TJ, Dorian, Darren and Holly, Colette, Patricia, Cheri, Gina, Jessica, Michelle, Denise, Ellen, Lacy, Rebecca J., Lisa, Heidi, Becky, Lea Ann, Michelle W., Julie, Kristin, Becky, Sabina, Anna, Leslie, Tosca, Sophie, Diane, Nicole, Jody, Tim, Susan W., Sandi, Cheryl, Randy, Patrick, Holly, Cyndi, Katy O., Katy G., Judy M.,

Erin, Jeanne, D'Ann, Liz, Caroline, Anita, Ralph, and Hope. I truly believe all Kingdom success of my books rests on your praying prowess.

Thank you, too, to the NGBC: Dr. Sandra Glahn, Kelley Mathews, and Rebecca Carrell, who have talked me through this book and whose scholarship I deeply appreciate. Thanks to Patrick, my husband, for talking through some of the theological implications for each overlooked woman in this text.

Jesus, thank you for not overlooking me, for dignifying me, for rescuing me in every possible way, and for empowering me to also see the overlooked. I love you.

Notes

Introduction

1 Bruce Hurt, "Acts 6 Commentary," Precept Austin, https://www.precept austin.org/acts-6-commentary.

Chapter One: Tamar, the Overlooked One

1 Megan Sauter, "Judah's Pledge to Tamar," Biblical Archaeology Society, October 27, 2021, https://www.biblicalarchaeology.org/daily/judahs -pledge-to-tamar/.
2 Ibid.
3 Editors, "Tamar," New World Encyclopedia, https://www.newworld encyclopedia.org/entry/Tamar. Originally quoted from Harold Bloom, *The Book of J* (New York, NY: Grove Press), 223.

Chapter Two: Miriam, the Unsung One

1 Mike Signorelli, "What Is Prophecy?," Mike Signorelli Ministries, https: //mikesignorelli.com/what-is-prophecy.

Chapter Three: Zelophehad's Daughters, the Overlooked Ones

1 Biblehub.com, https://biblehub.com/hebrew/4244.htm.
2 Biblehub.com, https://biblehub.com/hebrew/5270.htm.
3 Biblehub.com, https://biblehub.com/hebrew/2295.htm.
4 Biblehub.com, https://biblehub.com/hebrew/4435.htm.
5 Biblehub.com, https://biblehub.com/hebrew/8656.htm.
6 Bruce Hurt, quote from Ronald Allen, "Numbers 27 Commentary," Precept Austin, https://www.preceptaustin.org/numbers-27-commentary.
7 Ibid.
8 Editors, "Pistis," Bible Study Tools, https://www.biblestudytools.com /lexicons/greek/nas/pistis.html.

Chapter Four: Deborah, the Dismayed One

1 Albert Baylis, *From Creation to the Cross: Understanding the First Half of the Bible* (Grand Rapids, MI: Zondervan Academic, 2013), 173.
2 "Why Deborah Makes All the Difference," CBE International, originally a blog from The Center for Biblical and Theological Education at Seattle

Pacific University, https://www.cbeinternational.org/resource /why-deborah-makes-all-difference/.

Chapter Five: Abigail, the Trapped One

1 Bruce Hurt, "Nabal the Fool, a Son of Belial," 1 Samuel 25 Commentary, Precept Austin, https://www.preceptaustin.org/1-samuel-25-commentary #worth.

Chapter Six: Jehosheba, the Unnoticed One

1 Lauralyn Vasquez, "Jehosheba: How She Saved the Rightful King of Judah," Faithward, https://www.faithward.org/women-of-the-bible-study-series /jehosheba-how-she-saved-the-rightful-king-of-judah/.

Chapter Seven: Anna, the Unacknowledged One

1 Bruce Hurt, "Luke 2 Commentary," Precept Austin, updated February 11, 2023, https://www.preceptaustin.org/luke-2-commentary.
2 Ibid., (so BDAG 423 s.v. ewj 1.b.a).
3 Ibid., (so D. L. Bock, Luke [BECNT], 1:251–52; I. H. Marshall, Luke, [NIGTC], 123–24).
4 Ibid.

Chapter Eight: Martha, the Hurried One

1 Bruce Hurt, "Luke 10 Commentary," Precept Austin, updated July 30, 2023, https://www.preceptaustin.org/luke-10-commentary.
2 Ibid.
3 Oswald Chambers, "August 4," *My Utmost for His Highest* (New York: Dodd, Mead, & Co., 1924).

Chapter Nine: Lois and Eunice, the Older Ones

1 Abarim Publications, "Lois Meaning," https://www.abarim-publications .com/Meaning/Lois.html.
2 Abarim Publications, "Eunice Meaning," https://www.abarim-publications .com/Meaning/Eunice.html.
3 Bruce Hurt, "2 Timothy 1:5–6 Commentary," Precept Austin, updated November 18, 2022, https://www.preceptaustin.org/2_timothy_15-7.
4 Ibid.

Chapter Ten: Junia(s), the Misnamed One

1 For an outline of this controversy, see The Continuum, "Junia among the Apostles," October 3, 2008, https://anglicancontinuum.blogspot.com/2008/10/junia-among-apostles.html.
2 Marg Mowczko, "Junia: The Jewish Woman Who Was Imprisoned with Paul," Marg Mowczko blog, June 10, 2018, https://margmowczko.com/junia-jewish-woman-imprisoned/#_ftn11.
3 Bruce Hurt, "Romans 16:5–12 Commentary," Precept Austin, updated June 29, 2020, https://www.preceptaustin.org/romans_16_notes_pt2.
4 Marg Mowczko, "Junia in Romans 16:7," Marg Mowczko blog, April 1, 2010, https://margmowczko.com/junia-and-the-esv/.